The Efficient Kitchen

en

THE
AND
ERN
—A
HE
∴

THE EFFICIENT KITCHEN

The Efficient Kitchen

DEFINITE DIRECTIONS FOR THE
PLANNING, ARRANGING AND
EQUIPPING OF THE MODERN
LABOR-SAVING KITCHEN—A
PRACTICAL BOOK FOR THE
HOME-MAKER ∴ ∴ ∴ ∴ ∴ ∴

BY

GEORGIE BOYNTON CHILD

OF THE HOUSEKEEPING EXPERIMENT STATION
STAMFORD, CONN.

EDITED AND ARRANGED BY
LOUISE BOYNTON

NEW YORK
McBRIDE, NAST & COMPANY
1914

Copyright, 1914, by
GEORGIE BOYNTON CHILD

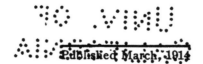
Published March, 1914

ane

DEDICATED
TO
MY THREE SISTERS
WHOSE LOVING COÖPERATION
HAS MADE POSSIBLE
THE WRITING OF
THIS BOOK

Introduction

TEN years ago my husband and I started home-making in a Western city. We had youth, ideals and a college education apiece; and while, like many other young people, we had no experience of married life, our early training as members of large families had given us a respect for practical work and a great love of home. After graduating from college I had kept house for two years for my father and mother, and for seven years had been business manager of a daily newspaper which my sister and I owned and ran. My husband was a technical chemist for a large Trust which had plants in different parts of the country.

Our income at the time was scarcely $1,300. But with a generous trousseau to solve the problem of clothes, and wedding presents to make our little home artistic and attractive, we were able to live very comfortably during the first year on less than $1,000.

We started our married life in one of the charming five-room cottages which have been so largely developed in Colorado and California, and which ease the physical burden of the care of the house in such a wonderful way. We had, even in those days, a washing machine, an electric iron, one of the labor-saving roasting pans, and several other efficient labor-saving devices. Therefore our housekeeping problems were reduced to the simplest possible proportions.

In the four years during which babies one, two and three arrived, we were fortunate in securing excellent help, and doubly fortunate in having our income increase to meet the extra expense involved. From that time on, however, with three babies to claim the lion's share of all my work and care, our living expenses jumped from less than $1,000 to $2,000 a year, without any change in our standard of living. During those years the cost of living began also to steadily advance, so that the purchasing power of the fixed income must be increased by constant study in buying more wisely and working more effectively. College and business training had taught me the advantage of systematic methods, of effective ways of arranging work and of diplomatic and considerate treatment of help. So our little home always ran smoothly. And when hard pulls came, as they often did, I had always the loving coöperation of my husband in overcoming them. We would take "shifts" with the night care of the babies, or he would run the washing machine for an hour before he went to work if the laundress failed me. Thus, like the noble Gareth, we were forced to win our knighthood through apprenticeship in "villain kitchen vassalage "; nor did we find it any undue hardship. Indeed had it lasted only for " a twelve-month and a day " this little book would never have been written.

But as the years went on and we moved East and lived in awkward, badly arranged Eastern houses, and tried to do efficient work in kitchens diabolically contrived to waste every human effort; as we found ourselves unable to get gas, for cooking in country houses, and did not know of any resource to take its place; as help of the right sort became almost impossible to secure; and as the " high cost of living " made constantly heavier demands upon us, we decided at last that we would have a Fourth of July, that we would make a great and final effort to free ourselves from the power of a tyrant that only seemed to tighten his hold the more sacrifices we made to his inordinate demands.

In this spirit we started on a determined quest for information and new resources. We took lessons in cooking to see whether the Domestic Science schools had any wonderful wisdom to impart in the direction of " better food for less money." We studied courses in Home Economics. We read books. We visited cooking laboratories and practise houses. Finally we came to the Housekeeping Experiment Station at Darien, Conn.

Here at last we found what we had been seeking: an inexpensive but charming home which had been so transformed by engineering skill that it

could be cared for with the minimum expense, and
so equipped that it could be operated with the smallest possible amount of effort.   Here we learned of
two wonderful resources for preparing food,
adapted to the income of the average home.   Here
we heard of Taylor's wonderful book on Scientific
Management, which has been revolutionizing the
business world.   And here we saw two old people
living happily an ideal life in which labor and culture each had its rightful place.   At last science
and high ideals had transformed " villain kitchen
vassalage " into the noble profession of home-making.

The resources which Mr. and Mrs. Barnard had
developed were suited to the needs of two people
living simply in the country, free from the demands
of city life, and free from all the subtle complica-
tions which constantly arise in larger households,
particularly in homes where there are little children.
But back of their work was a great idea, and this
idea was applicable to any home and to any income.
" Do not try to do efficient work in an inefficient
house. First transform your conditions."   This
is one of the first principles of engineering; and,
strange as it may seem, the very last principle applied in the average home.

By good fortune the opportunity came to us to
join Mr. Barnard in his work and to spend a year
in further study of equipment.   We must know
the best equipment for each kind of fuel, the equip-

ment which was best suited to the needs of the average home. We must work out better ideas in kitchen planning. And all this information must be catalogued and arranged so that it would be available to other home-makers.

While we were doing this work together we were constantly trying out new ideas, first at the Housekeeping Experiment Station, and then in other people's homes. At last we arrived at a simple system of coördination which we found could be adapted to every home and every condition. An interesting test of its efficiency was made when we were asked to plan a model kitchen for a Domestic Science Exhibition given in a large city.

All details were arranged in our office, and a list was sent covering directions for decoration and equipment. With this carefully grouped list in hand one of us went to the exhibition and in two hours had everything in place. Had the stove and sink been actually connected up a cook could have stepped in and served a very satisfactory dinner without loss of energy or time.

In the spring of 1911 Mr. Barnard retired from active participation in the Housekeeping Experiment Station.* His mantle fell on our younger shoulders. Through consultations and by means of lectures and pamphlets we have striven to make current his ideas on household economics, and those

* The Housekeeping Experiment Station is not open to visitors except for consultation and by appointment.

worked out by ourselves in association with him. But we have found that the help that the home-maker needed covered so wide a field that it was desirable to put the information first into book form, so that each subject could be studied in its relation to the whole problem.

" The Efficient Kitchen " is intended as a book of practical directions showing how to so build new kitchens or transform old ones that the work of the home may be accomplished with a sense of mastery, instead of remaining the hopeless problem it has become.

While it records only the beginning of a new science, and while it deals with only the practical matters, still we believe it will serve as a starting point from which every man and woman may gain the broad survey of resources through which alone a satisfactory solution of the home-making problem is possible. The rest of the problem consists of work and patient study, line upon line and precept upon precept, till the subject is mastered and success is attained.

Does the task seem toilsome and weary? It is no more so than mastering the technique of any art, or the rudiments of any profession. Let us give up the delusion that there is any higher work in life for man or woman than really mastering the problems of the home to which in common they owe allegiance. Let us face facts as they are. If ninety per cent of the home-makers in this country must

live on incomes that make domestic service prohib-
itory, let us hasten to transform our manner of
living so that we will not be carrying needless
financial burdens. The apprenticeship to "villain
kitchen vassalage" will not last forever. Intelligence will develop new resources, new methods of
doing work, better planned houses and better equipment. The home-maker will then have time to devote to the other side of life, to the things that bring
inspiration and joy and peace into this little circle
of love which we are proud to call "our home."

GEORGIE BOYNTON CHILD.

28 HOYT ST.,
STAMFORD, CONN.

CONTENTS

THE ILLUSTRATIONS

'Prince, thou shalt go disguised to Arthur's hall,
And hire thyself to serve for meats and drinks
Among the scullions and the kitchen knaves,
And those that hand the dish across the bar.
Nor shalt thou tell thy name to anyone.
And thou shalt serve a twelve month and a day.'

For so the Queen believed that when her son
Beheld his only way to glory lead
Low down thro' villain kitchen-vassalage,
Her own true Gareth was too princely-proud
To pass thereby; so should he rest with her,
Closed in her castle from the sound of arms.

Silent awhile was Gareth, then replied:
'The thrall in person may be free in soul,
And I shall see the jousts. Thy son am I,
And, since thou art my mother, must obey.
I therefore yield me freely to thy will;
For hence will I, disguised, and hire myself
.To serve with scullions and with kitchen-knaves;
Nor tell my name to any, no, not the King.'

Tennyson's " Idylls of the King."

THE EFFICIENT KITCHEN

I

THE FUNDAMENTAL PRINCIPLE

"WHAT *is* Algebra, Phœbe . . . exactly?" asks worried Miss Susan, in "Quality Street."

For many of us who aspire to be successful homemakers, some such dim aura of mystification clings round the wonderful new word *Efficiency*. How lightly it is bandied from mouth to mouth! What magical things it is said to do! Now it is offered us as a tempting bait. Again it is brandished over our heads as a club. We are to be Efficient, and to make our kitchens Efficient. And then, of course, our troubles will be at an end. But what has efficiency actually to do with *us?* How do we get it? What do we do with it? After all, exactly . . . what *is* Efficiency?

Mr. Charles Barnard has given the clearest definition of the term that we have seen. He says, "Efficiency has meant in the past the power to produce results. It now properly means much more. It means power to produce the best results at the lowest cost of time, labor and materials."

It has often seemed to us that Efficiency, like Boston, was " a state of mind." At any rate, it is the result of a certain flexibility of mind that commonly comes with culture and expert training, but that may also be gained by a right mental attitude toward the humble and arduous daily tasks that are ours. It is the very antithesis of the selfish and narrow individualism that insists upon considering every problem of the home as a " personal matter."

Women are not to be blamed for this. The conservatism, the somewhat petty insistence on individual preferences and prejudices that often seem reared like a solid wall in the way of progress in this important field, are but natural results of age-long repression. In general women have given the world what the world required of them — dumb acquiescence in things as they are. Now that something higher is required they will still respond. And they and the world will be the gainers. For the new gospel of Housekeeping Efficiency means that there is a *demand* for Housekeeping Efficiency; that the *efficiency* of women, their initiative and intelligence, are vitally needed if home life is to continue.

A preliminary, then, to planning our efficient kitchen, is the acquiring of an efficient attitude of mind. This implies liberation from bondage to outworn or merely personal habits and methods; a firm mental grasp of the *objects* of all our work; a firm faith that these right and necessary objects

can be achieved; above all a disposition to use merely
as *tools* the equipment, the circumstances and conditions that surround us.   These circumstances and
conditions, this income, be it large or small; this
wall-space, stove or egg-beater are just tools, to be
shifted about, changed, replaced or eliminated altogether, according as they serve or do not serve the
purpose for which they were intended.

This is what is meant by saying that efficiency
consists in *standardizing* work.   It is the difference
between what one individual can do, and the com-
posite result of the experience of many.

There is one best way to solve any given problem
of work.   We have seen the truth of this in play-
ing duplicate whist.   It is no longer the problem of
making the most of "*my* hand," but of making the
most of a hand that may come to *any* one, and
that will come to every one in turn in the game.
Whist players of unusual intelligence have studied
out certain *best* ways of proceeding when certain
given combinations of cards appear in a hand.
The amateur whist player profits by their study and
adopts the rules that have been found to bring results in the greatest number of cases.

The same holds true of the kitchen processes.
No matter how wide the difference between one
family and another in scale and manner of living,
by far the greater number of kitchen problems are
common to all kitchens, and there is *one best way* of
solving them.   To create an efficient kitchen is

therefore to *standardize* it; to work out, by a scientific study of the needs and conditions of the kitchen, the one best way of meeting each need; to work out certain standard principles of construction and grouping which shall best conform to universal requirements; to then show how this " standard type " may be adapted to meet the special requirements of those who have less than the normal amount of money to spend, or more than the normal amount of work to be done for the same amount of money.

To sum up, then: The problem that confronts us in the building and equipping of our kitchens is the developing of a standard type that will be adapted to the universal needs of the present day, and that can be modified to meet special needs without vital changes in the essential principles of construction and arrangement.

The title we have chosen for our book, "The Efficient Kitchen," expresses both the universal needs to be met, and the conditions governing the problem. The word *kitchen* suggests to each of us very much the same general round of tasks to be performed; and the word *efficient* expresses the need for getting results without wasted effort. This, too, is a universal requirement, because the pressure of life is now bearing very heavily upon us all. It is not only the tired little mother, striving to do all her work and care for two or three children on an insufficient income, who needs help; but the home-maker of abundant means, who has larger responsibilities and larger social and professional demands upon her income and her time. In the former case, the pressure to be lightened is physical strain; in the latter, an equally excessive and sometimes overwhelming mental strain.

There is one guiding principle which will enable us to solve a problem of this kind, and that is the principle of Conservation. Conservation is really the science of making the most of things. And to make the most of things we must have a very complete and exact knowledge of values. If we do not have a clear knowledge of values, we shall be continually sacrificing important things to unimportant or less important things, and shall not be conserving at all, but wasting.

Now, the housekeeping methods which have come down to us from our Colonial ancestors were all based on this same idea of conservation. Only our grandmothers had very different ideas as to what was worth while conserving. The values that loomed large in their eyes, were values that, at that time, cost the greatest amount of money. Food products that they could not produce themselves; manufactured articles of apparel which could not be woven or knitted at home, cost actual money; and money was not at all plentiful. Therefore they economized these costly values at the expense of time and human energy, which, then, were relatively cheap. They did not take into consideration fuel values, either, or consider large houses extravagant. Wood was plentiful; while the work necessary to prepare it for use, either for fuel or for building purposes, was done in the winter, when there was no market value for a man's time.

To-day conditions have entirely changed. Labor is dear, while manufactured articles are cheaper than ever before in the world's history. Commercial foods of certain kinds are comparatively cheap. In fact nearly everything that can be produced by machinery is cheap, and everything that must be done by hand is very high priced. Certain commodities that used to be abundant, and that consequently were of small money value, are now either growing scarce, or have been curtailed in production to artificially raise the price. Wood is much less abundant and is also subject to trust control. The coal supply is governed by a monopoly. Thus fuel which formerly was not even considered as an item of expense, is a very large expense to us to-day. We find the same change in the status of farm products. Eggs, butter, milk, chickens, pigs and fruit were all formerly produced by every householder, and were abundant and low-priced. All these commodities now have new values, and present new problems in relation to their use for food.

But the greatest of all shifting of values has come about in the new estimate of the value of a woman's work in the home. Fifty years ago the output of vitality and energy of even the most intelligent and highly organized women was a thing absolutely disregarded. The general attitude of mind on this subject can only be compared to that of the Southern farmer in whom an agricultural enthusiast tried to awaken an interest in the scientific feeding of his stock.

"You ought to give your pigs a warm mash instead of cold at this time of year," observed the expert.

"Why?" asked the farmer.

"Well," began the apostle of progress, "for one thing, a cold mash takes twice as much time to digest as food that is properly warmed."

"Does it?"

The proprietor of the pigs leisurely eyed his would-be benefactor, transferred his quid of tobacco from the right cheek to the left cheek, calmly spat, and finally remarked, "Say, Stranger, what do you reckon a hog's time is worth?"

Fifty years ago it seemed profitable and praiseworthy for the mother of a family to spend a whole winter making a rug of old "pants." It seemed worth while to spend hours each week mending stockings that required one or two hours patching a pair. Dishes that took an hour to prepare were concocted, merely to use up food materials that now would be thought of trifling value in comparison with the time taken to save them.

To-day all that has changed. For both men and women there are new standards of the worth of life and the value of human striving. But, in addition, woman's labor in the home has an actual market value, as those who are obliged to hire it have found out to their cost. It is worth, at a minimum, fifteen cents an hour for physical labor alone; and from that up to fifty cents, a dollar or even two dollars an hour for skilled or professional work. We find that the kind of mental energy that can coördinate, analyze and direct — that can " handle a situation," as it is termed in the world of achievement, is worth thousands of dollars a year in business and professional undertakings. Consequently we see that the problem of conserving this very expensive value in the home, outweighs in importance all the other factors in the home-making problem combined.

In business enterprises there has been an increasing tendency, during the last decade, toward conservation of the more valuable kinds of human energy by eliminating the causes of fatigue or waste of time. We know of one great concern which pays good salaries and requires efficient service of its clerks, both men and women. These clerks are expected to avail themselves, to the fullest extent, of the services of the office boy and stenographer, as well as of the labor-saving equipment of the office, so that their entire energies will be freed for the work of most value to the company. If a woman is employed at, say, $100 a month to keep certain records, she is supposed to spend her time on this work which is worth $100 a month, and for which she is trained. If she does errands or tele-

phoning which could be as well done by an office boy
worth $30 a month; or if she writes letters which
she could dictate to a stenographer in half the
time, she is considered as making a wasteful use of
time which belongs to the company.

While such a specialization of labor is impossible
in the average home, it is possible to conserve the
energy and time of the home-maker in an equally
effective way. This is accomplished by careful
planning and construction of the kitchen; by selecting labor-and-time-saving equipment; by grouping
the equipment in the way that will best promote effective, rapid work; and last of all by adopting an
efficient system which will help to reduce all the
mechanical parts of the work to automatic processes,
In this way the fresh thought and energy of the
housekeeper is saved for the most important part of
home-making, the exercise of loving care that
watches over every essential affecting the welfare
of the home circle. This is more a problem of wise
administration than of routine housekeeping. It
calls for love, intelligence and expert training.
Very often women who are abundantly endowed
with the right thought and intelligence to make the
most perfect kind of homes have not had the training to master the technique and are discouraged by
its complexity. There are so many homely facts
to be reckoned with, so much apparently unimportant detail to be covered, that the task seems hopeless. So they drift along and let their lives and

their home-making be controlled by circumstance. All that is needed to transform such homes is a willingness to look at the problem from a different point of view; to see that mastery of the work we have chosen is the first step to a self-mastery that vitally affects our character, that will do much toward creating right ideals in our children, and that will do more for the world at large than any work outside the home, however brilliant, if undertaken at the expense of the responsibilities we assumed when we started out in married life.

This little book has been written for home-makers, men as well as women. Its theme is mastery of the practical difficulties that are summed up in the phrase "the technique of housekeeping." Its object is to awaken interest in a constructive solution of such problems, which will result, directly, in freedom and independence; and indirectly in a new spirit of joy and peace. Such men and women understand that housekeeping processes are merely means to an end. They know that efficiency is not gained simply by making the work-room efficient, but that it is a way of thinking, an attitude of mind, that involves mental mastery. They are ready to see work in its proper relation to life, to learn to subordinate the unessential to the essential, to think clearly and logically and to get results.

Very few home-makers can go to school again to get the mental training so essential to success. But we must remember that the greatest teachers and thinkers of the world got their own education in the school of experience. Rightly viewed and rightly used the kitchen is not a bad training school. It presents problems in organization and administration as complex as any to be found in business. It gives a field for as great skill in chemical combinations as is to be met with in many a scientific laboratory. Its opportunities for scientific investigation are as varied as those of the Rockefeller or Pasteur Institutes. Only the titles and emoluments seem lacking.

To-day most of us are content to feel that we are doing a difficult and important task well. But there will undoubtedly come a time when the more ambitious home-maker will be able to write after her name titles as imposing as Master of Science or Doctor of Laws. Perhaps by that time some such title will be more highly regarded than those showing scientific attainments only. For the day is coming when the test of the value of scientific attainments will be their power to enhance the value of practical living. One thing is sure. She who shall have solved the problem of successful home-making, will have been obliged to bring to her work as much intelligence and training as is required by any other science or profession.

II

Planning the Kitchen

MUCH of the modern housekeeper's distress is due to the fact that our kitchens express the needs and customs of our grandmothers' time, and not those of to-day.

Less than a hundred years ago the home itself produced what the family consumed, and sheltered many workers. The kitchen was then the workroom of the house and was necessarily large, as it was the scene of many and varied industries. Sewing, knitting, quilting; candle-making, and preparing food on a large scale for winter consumption, were all carried on in one big room. Living was very simple, social demands very few. And large houses and open country expressed the restful sense of "room to breathe in." Weariness then came more from physical work than from any pressure on nerves and brain due to the character of the work or its conditions.

To-day nearly all the old-time industries have been banished from the home and put on a commercial footing, in many cases to the detriment of the home-maker. We buy our clothing and our canned fruit. Instead of making candles we switch on the electric light. The kitchen is a place where food is prepared, and where practically nothing else is done. The physical strain of the old days has been succeeded by an even greater mental strain, due to the great expensiveness of everything we use in our homes, and to the continual necessity of dealing with conditions outside the home which we cannot control. There is no margin left for mistakes or extravagance, whether of time, of strength or of money. Efficient kitchens, such as insure to the worker proper rest, economy of the vital forces, have become an absolute necessity.

It is this need for economy of nerve force, this new need peculiar to an age of high pressure and rapid mental readjustment, that our kitchen must be equipped to meet. Efficiency must be the keynote. Efficient work. Efficient rest. Elimination of all unnecessary work. The doing of necessary work in the easiest and most economical way. These are the problems of every home-maker, whether rich or poor; whether she have one servant, or none, or several. Even if she performs no part of the work of the kitchen herself she must, in these days of untrained help and shifting economic conditions, give her kitchen constant supervision, if she is to realize her dream of creating the ideal home.

In meeting the new conditions no single change has proved so helpful as the passing of the old-fashioned " roomy " kitchen of fond memory, and the adoption of the very modern and utilitarian small kitchen.

Where space is restricted a most careful study is, of course, necessary in order to make the most of the space at one's command. But when such a study has been made, when the kitchen is a compact and truly efficient work-room, the saving in time, strength and labor due to the simple elimination of useless space, is almost incalculable. In the small kitchen there is less wall and floor space to be gone over in the daily care and cleaning. The concentration of all the working processes near together and in convenient relation to one another, saves hours of time by preventing useless steps and awkward, unnecessary motions. Moreover, the small kitchen means great economy in construction — a very important matter in these days when building is so costly. Every square foot of flooring and partition cut out of the kitchen where it is not needed may be added with advantage to some other part of the house where extra space means added health, comfort and opportunity for the entire family.

We assume, therefore, that the housekeeper will have a small kitchen if she can; or will limit her remodeled kitchen to the smallest possible dimensions. We will proceed to consider how this limited space may be used to the best advantage.

USES THE KITCHEN MUST SERVE

The final plans for the kitchen must be drawn by an architect. It is not the purpose of this book to give any information that comes under the head of technical construction. Its object is, rather, to call attention to the various *uses* which the kitchen must serve, and of which many good architects are woefully ignorant.

It is a very interesting thing to notice the working out of thought. If we begin by holding steadfastly in mind the *object* to be gained, some way will be found of overcoming difficulties and achieving the desired result. If, on the other hand, we allow ourselves, too early in the planning process, to be diverted by a consideration of ways and means, we are apt to land in discouragement and hopeless confusion.

Therefore, first of all, before we begin to think of details, or even picture to ourselves the general outline of the room, we must think of the work to be done in the room. We remember the four main requisites of all kitchens: storage place for supplies, including refrigeration; a work table on which to prepare the food; proper arrangements for cooking; the water supply, including facilities for dishwashing and cleaning up. These are fundamental needs, and must be met in any kind of kitchen for a family of any size.

The next consideration is that the kitchen conveniences be in compact relation to one another, so as to economize the workers' time and strength. Most of us know that kitchen work is not a series of isolated tasks, but that one task must be fitted in with another most ingeniously if we are to do anything like an effective day's work. Therefore our supplies, our work table, our stove and our sink must be near enough together so that we can " keep an eye" on one thing while we are doing other things. We wash the breakfast dishes while we watch the cake baking. We cook the cereal for next morning's breakfast while we wash the supper dishes. We realize that we can work easily and effectively just in proportion as we use skill in planning and arranging our work.

Having coördinated our working processes, we picture to ourselves the right conditions in which to work. We must have plenty of light, both day-times and evenings. The light must fall on our work and not shine in our eyes. The kitchen must be well ventilated, comfortably warmed in winter and cool in summer. All possible provision must be made for doing the work in reasonable comfort and without useless expenditure of the workers' time and strength.

We next remember that, besides the immediate needs of the work itself, there are other require-ments to be met in the kitchen. A place for wraps and rainy-day things. Some safe depository for in-coming supplies. We decide to make a list of all the kitchen needs we can think of, jotting them down roughly, like this:

1. Work table and its accessories, including containers for groceries used in mixing.
2. Sink and its outfit.
3. Stove and its accessories.

4. Containers and special working shelf for cutting bread, cake, pastry, etc.
5. Provision for keeping food cold. Refrigerator. Cold closet.
6. Provision for keeping food warm and drying dishes.
7. Arrangements for heating the water supply.
8. Arrangements for heating the kitchen.
9. Drawers for cutlery, kitchen linen, aprons, etc.
10. Place for cleaning preparations, and cleaning cloths.
11. Shelf or closet for incoming supplies.
12. Place for broom, mops, etc.
13. Closet for wraps.
14. Laundry arrangements, if no provision can be made for these in a separate room.

Up to this point the planning has been quite a simple matter, because we have been thinking of the kitchen as a work-room by itself and not in its relation to other parts of the house. The complexities begin just here. Not only must the kitchen be rightly placed in relation to the dining-room and rear entrance; but its plumbing and heating and flue connections must be planned with reference to the house systems and must conform to these to a certain degree, in order not to cause unnecessary expense. Then we begin to find things conflicting and interfering with one another. Our simple, convenient arrangement of sink and stove and work table may prove impracticable. Flues go here, where we wanted to put our sink. Pipes go there in that excellent place for a work table. Doors and windows, apparently, must fill all the wall spaces so desirable for open-shelf cupboards. Our kitchen seems verging on a mere conglomeration of exits and entrances; of wires and pipes and flues.

It is just at this point that the woman who is determined to have a convenient kitchen is apt to find herself in conflict with the architect.   Just here she will realize the wisdom of having thought out the *ends* the kitchen must serve, rather than the *means* by which those ends may be attained.   The starting point of all successful architecture is *use;* that which a room or a building or a bridge or a factory is *for*.   The reason why so many gifted architects fail in kitchen construction is simply because they have only the most rudimentary ideas, or none at all, of the actual requirements of a modern kitchen.   These the home-maker knows.   And this knowledge she must be able to impart to the architect if he needs it.   She must be prepared to stand her ground very firmly when told that this or that structural necessity interferes with the vital convenience of arrangement.   She cannot stubbornly insist that the sink shall go *here* and the work table *there*.   But she can explain clearly that this, that and the other need is imperative in the kitchen; that such and such kitchen processes must be coordinated.   Once he clearly understands the end in view a competent architect will find means to bring this about.

If we plan our kitchen before we plan any other room in the house almost all these difficulties can be mastered very easily.   If we leave it until the last it will require just that much more ingenuity to accomplish our purpose.   But one thing we must keep steadfastly in mind. The legitimate needs of kitchen construction can and will be met, provided the home-maker herself knows clearly what they are. On her realization of this, and her patient determination to make others realize it, depends much of the future success of her home.

CHOICE OF METHODS AND MATERIALS

After having, in conference with the architect, worked out the structural plan of an efficient kitchen, the home-maker will find herself at every stage of the work, required to make choices between this or that method or material; this or that alternative in working out some detail of construction. On her wise decision of all these points depends the convenience of the kitchen as a work-room; the cost of building and equipping the kitchen; and above all the cost of maintenance after it has been built and equipped. She must therefore know what the possibilities are, and what the result of her choice in each case is going to be.

Two general principles will guide her safely. The first applies to choice of materials. Get only what is good of its kind. If you cannot afford the best, do not get a cheap substitute, but choose something less expensive, which is still the best of its kind. In kitchen wall finish, for example, a good grade of rough plaster, tinted, is better than a poor grade of hard-trowel finished plaster, painted. A reliable mason will estimate on either. But poor work of the more expensive grade should not be accepted.

The second general principle applies to the choice of contractors to carry out the work planned. Get only men of known reputation to estimate on your contract. If you find you cannot afford to get the house well built as planned, do not accept a cheaper estimate from a less reliable man. Eliminate every unnecessary thing and have good work as far as you go. There are too many ways of being cheated in materials and workmanship to make it wise to take any chances.

DETAILS OF KITCHEN CONSTRUCTION

Size of the Kitchen.

The convenience and economy of the small kitchen have been referred to at the beginning of this chapter. We are realizing the need of many things in the home which are more to be desired than unnecessary space in the kitchen. Sun parlors, outdoor dining-rooms and maids' sitting-rooms are beginning to seem necessities, and in very many cases could be afforded if no space were wasted on rooms where space is not required. A small upstairs laundry and pressing-room is another need that must often be met in the housekeeping of to-day. A very convenient kitchenette can be made of a room seven feet by eleven. We recommend this size for a family without a maid, or where only one house-worker is employed. Convenient dimensions for the aver-

age family are ten by twelve feet, or eleven by thir-
teen.   The kitchen ought to be oblong rather than
square to get the best result of wall space.

*Relation of Kitchen to Dining-Room and Outside
Porch.*

Very often, in order to save expense in construc-

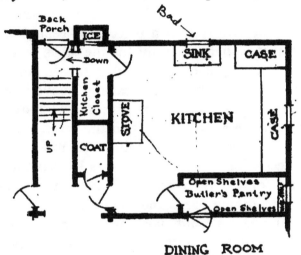

DINING ROOM

FIG. 1.— Floor plan showing indirect connection between
kitchen and back door and kitchen and dining room.

tion the kitchen opens directly from the dining-room
by means of a swinging door.   It is better, however, to have a small pantry between.   (See simplest type butler's pantry, Fig. 1.)   This pantry
gives wonderful storage facilities, prevents odors
from passing from the kitchen to the dining-room,
and deadens the noise between the two rooms.   It
may be small or large, but if rightly planned every

inch of wall space may be made available. A working shelf twenty to twenty-eight inches wide and thirty-two inches from the floor may be built around two or three sides of the pantry. Under this, shallow drawers may be built in to hold dining-room supplies, or kitchen supplies that cannot be kept in the kitchen. This wide shelf may be stained and varnished, or it may be covered with zinc. It ought to be left free as a place for keeping salads, desserts, etc., that are ready for the table, or to provide a working-place for making salads and sandwiches, or cutting bread and cake. Above it should be narrow open shelves for dishes. This arrangement is far less expensive than the wide-shelf cupboards with glass doors, will hold more and be more accessible. A pantry of this kind is the ideal location for the refrigerator, making it equally accessible to dining-room and kitchen.

The kitchen should have, wherever possible, an indirect connection with the outer door. This prevents much tracking in of dirt, and saves the worker from needless interruption. The advantages of this plan are illustrated in Fig. 1.

Whatever arrangement is made, care should be taken to have the outer door so placed that the kitchen will be protected from the cold winter winds. The north opening found in many homes makes the kitchen a bleak place in cold weather. If the door itself faces north the entrance porch should be partly enclosed and given a more favorable exposure.

A well arranged and well equipped kitchen, New Rochelle, N. Y.

Butler's pantry and dining-room, New Rochelle, N. Y. Refrigerator in pantry has outside icing door. Ornamental slide above sideboard opens into butler's pantry

Arrangement of Windows.

Good light and good ventilation are secured by having enough windows and having them rightly placed.   They ought to be so placed as to make a

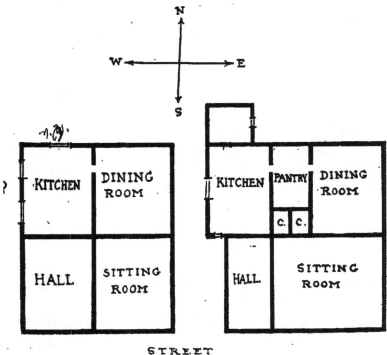

STREET

FIG. 2.   FIG. 3.

cross draft possible.   In most kitchens two windows are enough.   If they are built in opposite or adjoining walls, good ventilation will also be assured.

Suppose a house of the simplest possible construction.   (See Fig. 2.)   In this the kitchen is the northwest room.   The rear door opens toward the north. There is no place for windows except in the west wall. By building the kitchen with a slight jog or L, as shown in Fig. 3, and enclosing the rear door with a vestibule or storm door opening east, the following advantages are secured:

The kitchen is given cross draft west and south. Its two windows in adjoining walls give better light than if both were placed in the same wall. The few feet of extra width render possible a narrow pantry between the kitchen and dining-room. The vestibule or storm door at the back protects the kitchen from the North wind.*

The additional expense will be more than repaid by the extra comfort and efficiency of the kitchen. In case of a very narrow margin for expense it would be worth while to slightly reduce the scale of the entire house to allow for this important advantage in construction.

If both windows must be in the same wall, as sometimes happens, then there should be a ventilating register in the opposite wall or a transom over the kitchen door leading to the porch or vestibule. Windows and doors should never be so located as to badly break up the wall space. It requires care in planning to avoid this; but the extra trouble is well worth while.

It is also a good plan to have the windows placed higher in the kitchen than in the other rooms, so

* The great comfort in summer of a direct draft through the kitchen from North to South would be secured by having a window in the vestibule on the North side.

that if necessary, a table or sink may be placed underneath. A good height for the lower sill is 3½ feet from the floor. Sometimes cross ventilation can be accomplished by extending the kitchen wall beyond the outline of the rest of the house.

Ventilation.

Under ordinary conditions good ventilation will be secured by the proper location of the windows and outer door. In addition to this there must be the right flue connection for gas or coal stove. Gas stoves are often installed without flue connection, but it is a bad practice. The best arrangement is to have the gas range connected with a flue and a hood above. A ventilating register placed under the hood will carry off all unpleasant odors. The cost of such an arrangement is about twelve dollars.

Chimney Flues, Gas Pipes and Water Pipes.

Where a coal range is to be used a separate flue must be provided for it in building the chimney. Very often the same flue is used for both the kitchen range and the dining-room fireplace, with very disappointing results. Improper draft makes it impossible to get good service from a coal range. And where the flue is shared with the kitchen range, the fireplace is very apt to smoke. Each flue compartment should be at least eight by eight inches.

The location of chimney flues, gas pipes and water pipes in the kitchen must be worked out in connection with the general plan of the house systems. If the housekeeper explains to the architect the special needs that must be met in the kitchen he can make these systems conform to meet her needs. But it is a difficult matter to do this if the general house plans have been worked out before the designing of the kitchen is begun. The needs of the kitchen are of such vital importance that it is well worth while to make these the starting point.

Artificial Lighting.

In the lighting of the kitchen the matter of chief importance is to provide for *enough* light. Where electricity is used one kitchen bulb centrally located and equipped with a Tungsten globe of sixty Watts, will give ample light for a small kitchen. For a larger room two will be needed, and ought to be so placed that the stove and sink are both well lighted. If gas is used, the gas jets should be equipped with mantles and chimneys, and the mantles renewed when necessary.

For country kitchens alcohol bracket lamps give a more brilliant light than kerosene and require much less care. The ordinary alcohol lamp, burning denatured alcohol and equipped with a mantle, gives a forty-five candle-power light. The chimneys never get sooty and need only occasional washing to keep the glass clear. Denatured alcohol may be purchased by the barrel for approximately forty cents a gallon.

Kerosene is much less expensive than alcohol if the cost in money alone is considered. Kerosene lamps may now be purchased with mantles. Great improvement has been made in their manufacture. The smell of kerosene on the hands, however, makes the care of these lamps an unpleasant task. And the care necessary is no small item. Daily cleaning and washing of chimneys is required, with frequent renewing of wicks in order to get good results and prevent the lamps from giving off an unpleasant odor while burning.

Finish of Walls and Ceiling.

There are almost as many grades of plaster finish on the market in these days as there are kinds of eggs. In olden times an egg not absolutely above suspicion was a bad egg. To-day we have all grades from " strictly fresh " to " boxed eggs." Every grade, in fact, except downright bad eggs. These are sold without labels. In the same way plaster of all grades is now offered the credulous customer. It is a difficult matter to get the permanent, hard-finished plaster which is the only kind worth having on the walls. It is particularly important to have this grade of plaster in the kitchen. The only way to secure it is by having the work done by the most reliable mason you know and paying the price.

There are two finishes which can be recommended, each having its advantages. The first is the smooth, hard-trowel finish, which is best if the walls are to be painted. Such a finish is very clean and sanitary. It needs wiping over occasionally with a damp flannel cloth fastened around a broom; and should have a thorough washing once a year to remove the more permanent stains. This is hard work, especially for the upper part of the walls and the ceiling. For this reason many prefer the rough tinted finish which can be kept clean by wiping off once a month, and be freshened once a year by a new coat of tint. When this finish is selected the tinting is done in the first instance by mixing the tint with the final coat of plaster. The yearly tinting is no more expensive than the paint-washing.

Treatment of Old Kitchen Walls.

In the case of old kitchens, one must be guided by the condition of the walls. If these are well preserved, the ceiling and upper half of the wall may be tinted and the lower half painted a color to exactly match the tint. This treatment may also be used for new walls where it is desirable to give the wainscoting a more permanent finish than a tinted surface. One firm makes a tint and paint to match. Care must be taken to properly remove the old finish before applying the new.

Cost of Wall Finish.

It is impossible to give more than a rough estimate of the cost of wall finishes. Decorators of experience tell us that the difference in plaster finish makes it impossible to give general estimates. One wall will absorb three times as much kalsomine or paint as another will require. There are also different grades of workmanship. One contractor gave the range of prices for kalsomining, including labor and material, at from three cents to a dollar and a half per square yard! The difference was largely due to difference in workmanship. The same difference prevails in painting, prices ranging from four cents per square yard to a dollar and twenty cents. In the case of kalsomine the expense for material is very little, and for ordinary work does not require skilled labor. Often it can be done by a member of the household.

The cost of materials is, approximately, as follows:

Kalsomine, one to three coats, cost per square yard, one cent each coat.

Paint, one to two coats, cost per square yard, four and a half cents each coat.

Washable oilcloth paper, one and a half yards wide, cost per yard, 26 cents.

The number of coats of kalsomine needed depends upon the kind of plaster and the condition of the walls. At least two are usually necessary. If the wall is cracked the cracks should be filled with plaster of Paris and touched up with shellac before putting on the kalsomine.

New surfaces require at least two coats of paint. Two are usually enough unless the grain of the wood is pronounced and it is to be painted white.

Two coats are necessary where paint is put on over a darker color. If there is little change in color one coat will be enough.

Flat paints that are washable cover more surface than the oil paints, and are much used for that reason. The cost of labor in different localities and for different grades of work varies greatly. The ordinary price is four dollars to four and a half per day.

Wall paper should never be put on kitchen walls. The only exception to this is the washable oil-cloth paper, which is recommended where the walls are in bad condition and need strengthening. This paper comes in various colors for the side walls, with ceiling paper to correspond. The gloss finish is the best for kitchen use, although the choice of colors and patterns is more limited than in the "tinted" and "mercerized" finish. As stains often get on the kitchen walls which require more than wiping off these more attractive finishes cannot be recommended. This paper comes a yard and a half wide and costs 26 cents a yard.

An ideal finish for the side walls of the kitchen is glazed tile. The cost, however, is prohibitive for the average home, being sixty to seventy-five cents per square foot. Tiling may be used for the baseboard and half-way up the wall, the upper part being painted. This is a very satisfactory and permanent finish.

The Kitchen Floor.

For the average home a well-laid kitchen floor covered with inlaid linoleum will give the most satisfactory result for the amount of money spent. The best grade of linoleum costs from $1.60 to $1.75 per square yard, and if properly laid and cared for will last twenty years. The flooring beneath need not be hard wood, but it must be evenly laid. If it is not even it should be made so before laying the linoleum.

To lay a linoleum well is the work of an expert and should never be attempted by the amateur. Whenever it is possible, have the firm that furnishes and lays the linoleum, take the measurements also. Very accurate measurements are required. And if a mistake is made it is well to be in a position to hold the dealers responsible. The price for laying the linoleum covers taking the measurements, cutting and laying, and a third trip a month later, after the linoleum has had time to "stretch" to tack it in position. In the city the charge for this work is usually ten cents a square yard. For out-of-town homes four or five dollars and traveling expenses is charged. This price includes the time required for the three trips, but does not include railroad fares.

If in spite of every precaution the linoleum should "buckle" the firm should be promptly notified so that the trouble may be rectified at once. Even the best grade will soon wear out if these ridges are allowed to remain.

If water is allowed to get under the surface of linoleum it causes serious damage. For this reason great care should be taken in wiping up. And water spilled on it should not be allowed to remain. An excellent precaution is to cement the edges together, where piecing is necessary. It may also be cemented round the edges. The best plan is to have a half inch, quarter-round molding tacked to the side wall just above the edge of the linoleum. Never nail the molding *through* the linoleum. This covers the open space allowed for stretching and makes a neat finish.

It is not necessary that the flooring underneath the linoleum be of hard wood. It will save expense to use a good grade of cheap, strong North Carolina pine. The best width for flooring is two or two and a half inch. The cost of such wood when purchased of a reliable firm which thoroughly kiln-dries its flooring is about four cents per square foot. This is for the seven-eighths-inch flooring, which wears better than the half-inch. For a cost of two to three cents more per square foot one may secure the best grade of edge-grained North Carolina pine or clear maple flooring. These two latter floorings may be used without linoleum. They should be stained and treated to two coats of special floor varnish, and then be kept waxed. This makes an excellent floor, but is not as comfortable to stand on or as easily cared for as the linoleum. In estimating the cost of flooring, as the material is tongued and grooved, it will be necessary to allow twenty-five per cent more than the actual area to be covered by the North Carolina pine; and thirty-five per cent more for the maple. For 100 square feet of floor space, for example, one would need 125 square feet of North Carolina pine; or 135 square feet of maple. The cost of laying and scraping such a floor will ordinarily be about four cents per square foot, but may be much higher in certain localities.

Oiling kitchen floors is not to be recommended. For other parts of the house an oiled floor, when properly done, is very satisfactory. But in the kitchen it is difficult to care for because stains are so hard to remove. It is very important to have the kitchen floor comfortable to stand on, easy to keep clean, and durable. For all these reasons hard-wood floors are not as desirable for the kitchen as linoleum.

Under certain conditions other floor coverings are preferred to linoleum. Where great economy must be exercised in building and outfitting, the painted floor may be selected. Two coats of good floor paint in tan or gray are attractive in appearance and wear fairly well. When worn spots appear they should be touched up at once. If the floor is not hard-wood it should be given two coats of shellac before the paint is applied, and all cracks should first of all be

filled with crack filler. For laying such a floor the
cost of lumber and labor will be about eight cents
per square foot; the cost of paint and labor about
two cents per square foot. The painting may be
done at home. Some home-makers get very expert
with the use of the paint brush.

. Many kitchens in newly built homes have cement
floors. The different cement preparations are called
by various names, but are very much alike in their
general properties. It is a matter of considerable
skill to lay them; and unless well laid they crack
and are easily disfigured. These floors have base-
boards continuous with the flooring and are ideal
for purposes of keeping clean. If porches, halls,
and entrances have this flooring, as well as the
kitchen, the cost is not prohibitive. The firms
usually quote a price of about twenty-five cents per
square foot, where three hundred and fifty square
feet are laid at one time. This is because it is
necessary to send out experts especially to do the
work, and it costs nearly as much to execute small
orders as larger ones. An extra charge of thirty
cents per lineal foot is made for a four-inch sanitary
base board laid at the same time. The foundations
under the flooring must meet certain requirements
in order to have this price apply. These floorings
come in tan, deep red, mottled and green. The
mottled is a very good kitchen color. The tans and
reds are recommended because the colors run evenly.
The green is by far the prettiest for porches. The

only serious objection to the cement flooring for kitchen use is that it is not restful to stand on.   This may be obviated by having rubber or washable rugs in front of the sink and work table.

The natural cement floors are not attractive in appearance and crack unless carefully laid.   The colored preparations are therefore to be preferred.

Tile flooring of the vitrified kind makes a very attractive looking floor.   But it is hard on the feet, " death to china " and costs about forty cents a square foot.

Treatment of Wood-work in Kitchens.

Hard wood is more important for the wood-work of the kitchen than in any other room in the house. The kitchen wood-work gets such hard wear, and needs so much cleaning, that a permanent and sanitary finish is the ideal one.   An inexpensive hard-wood that can be treated with a turpentine stain and then waxed, makes an excellent finish.   Equally durable is the varnish finish, but the effect is not so good.

By far the most attractive finish for wood-work is white enamel paint.   For a new kitchen, if this is to be the finish, the wood must be selected with great care.   Some kinds of wood have such a decided grain that four or five coats of white are necessary to cover them up.   The best wood for this purpose is white wood, which will require but two coats of paint, and one coat of enamel.   This finish must have daily care, and will need renewing in two or three years. It is therefore not to be recommended for households where labor must be economized, or where the expense of renewing would be a serious matter.

Kitchen wood-work that has become shabby may be treated with two coats of tan or gray paint. This helps wonderfully in giving a fresh and clean appearance to an old kitchen. But it must be treated with care, frequently touched up and renewed when necessary. For this reason a hard wax or varnish finish is to be preferred wherever it is possible to have it.

III

Scientific Grouping

A MOST efficient means of conserving the worker's time and strength is found in the new scientific method of grouping the various utensils and materials, not according to kind, but according to the uses they serve.

In most kitchens groceries are kept together in one closet; agate-ware utensils in another; cooked food in still another; service dishes which are part of a set, in the dining-room. This is a logical arrangement, and we do not see that it is wasteful of labor until we begin to work. Then we find that the waste of steps involved in getting equipment and material together for any one process becomes a very serious loss indeed, not only of the time but of the energy of the worker. We see that if we are to conserve labor and energy we must adopt a plan of grouping that will coördinate utensils and materials as they are needed for the actual work to be done.

Before discussing the new theory, let us analyze two simple processes repeated every day in the kitchen, and see how laborious is the old way of getting them accomplished, as a result of the wrong method of grouping. The first is the very simple task of making tea. As freshly boiled water is a necessity for good tea, our first step is to empty and partly refill the tea-kettle, or get a small stew-pan and cover and boil water enough for our tea on the stove. This will mean two trips if the tea-kettle is used; and four if we must get a stew-pan from a closet, a cover from the rack, and go to the sink to fill our utensil, and then to the stove to boil the water. Next, while the water is boiling, we go to the china closet and get the teapot, to the shelf where groceries are kept for the tea, to the dining-room for. cups, saucers, spoons and sugar bowl. Then we make the tea. We have made in the first case, five trips about the room in order to get our materials together; in the second case, where a small saucepan and cover are used, seven trips. Compare the great waste of labor in this simple process, with the ease of making tea by the new method. In this latter case we have the entire tea-making outfit grouped near the sink. We stand at the sink and reach for the stew-pan or tea-kettle, and fill it with water, take two steps to the stove and put the water on to boil. The pot-covers are just back of the stove. The teapot and tea canister are on a shelf above the sink, and cups, saucers and spoons are placed beside them. In making our tea this second time we have moved perhaps five feet in all, and cut in two the labor and effort required to do the work. In the former case we had to make five or seven trips to different parts of the kitchen and dining-room, and probably walk at least twenty-five feet, in order to accomplish the self-same task.

Another very simple task performed at least three times a day is the cutting of bread. With the bread box on the table in the pantry, the bread knife in the cutlery drawer, the bread board hanging up against an opposite kitchen wall, we must make three separate trips in order to get our materials together and prepare to do the work.

Every separate task or process that we analyze shows the same wastefulness of labor and time, due to the fact that our kitchen outfit and supplies are wrongly coördinated. We begin to realize how serious is this waste when we remember that very many of the kitchen tasks are performed three times a day; and that the number of separate processes carried on each day in even the simplest kitchen is between twenty-five and a hundred. It is no exaggeration to say that at least two hours a day are lost in the average kitchen by improper grouping of supplies and utensils. Where servants are kept and the living is elaborate it often requires the services of an extra maid to make up for the lack of efficient arrangement. It is therefore clear that the new idea must be applied to every detail from the original laying out of the kitchen, the locating of the sink, stove and work table, to properly sub-dividing the most insignificant of the kitchen tools. On this basis we proceed to group the utensils around the fixed equipment to which they belong, which gives a grouping like the following:

Articles to be grouped near the range:

Salt Box.	Match Box.
Flour Dredger.	Empty Box for Matches.
Pepper Dredger.	Stove Cloths.
Pot Covers.	Asbestos Mats
Frying Pans.	Griddle (in Winter time).
Dripping Pans.	Rack for Dish Towels.

Articles to be grouped near the sink:

Dish Pan.
Dish Drainer.
Rubber Sink Stopper.
Three-foot Rubber Tubing with thread connection.

Cleaning outfit to be grouped near sink:

Sink Solutions.
Scouring Soap.
Corn Meal for Care of Hands.
Bay-Rum Lotion for Hands.

Group on shelf above sink:

Teapot and Tea Canister.	Pitchers, Assorted Sizes.
Percolator and Coffee Canister.	Stew Pans (either on shelf or suspended from wall below).
Double Boiler.	

Suspend from edge of shelf or wall back of sink the following small implements:

Soap Shaker.	Vegetable Brush.
Soap Dish.	Bottle-Cleaning Brush.
Dish Mop.	Small Funnel.
Sink Shovel.	Small Wire Strainers.
Wire Whisk Sink Brush.	Plate Scrapers.
	Pot Scraper.

Place in open-shelf cupboard near sink:

Outfit of Dishes for Left-Over Food
  6 Small Agate Pans.
  4 Agate Pans, 2 to 3 quart Capacity.
  6 Agate Plates.
  4 Larger Agate Plates.
Kitchen China as Required by Size of Family.

At right of sink have nickel towel-bar for hand towel, or a roll of paper toweling. If possible have a drawer near sink where may be kept a supply of kitchen towels, wash cloths and cheese-cloth for straining.

We then plan to group the supplies and utensils used in preparing food so that no extra steps will have to be taken to assemble them for each cooking operation. This gives us a grouping like the following near the work-table:

Articles to be grouped near work table:

2 Measuring Cups.
4 Small White + Yellow Bowls.
Yellow Mixing Bowls.
2 Baking Dishes, 2-pint and 3-pint sizes.
Rolling Pin.
Pastry Board.
Pie Plates.
Cake Mixer.
Cake Tins, Various Kinds.
Muffin Tins.
Cutters for Cookies, Dough-nuts, etc.
Bread Mixer.
Flour Sifter.
Liquid Shortening.
Bread Pans.
Meat Grinder.
Crank Beater.

Puree Strainer.
Containers for Spices.
Jars for Grocery Supplies.
Containers for Flour, Sugar, Rice, and Cereals.
Cutlery Outfit
  1 dozen teaspoons.
  4 to 6 kitchen knives.
  4 to 6 kitchen forks.
  4 to 6 table-spoons.
  A good meat knife.
  Spatula.
  Apple Corer.
  2 Vegetable Knives.
  Outfit of Measuring Spoons.
  Scissors.
  Mixing Spoons.
  Wooden Spoons.
  Egg Beater.

We shall find certain other utensils that require special shelves or closets, on account of their size; and certain outfits that are used constantly in some kitchens and not at all in others. We group these in the following:

Special list:

Steamers.	Outfit for Deep-fat Frying
Portable Oven.	Frying Basket.
Waffle Iron.	Scotch Kettle.
Toaster.	Pail for Frying-fat.

A salad outfit in the average family would include: Salt shaker, pepper shaker, paprika, garlic cloves, vinegar bottle, oil bottle.

In every kitchen where there is no pantry between kitchen and dining-room, a special place must be provided for the bread box, bread board and bread knife. Also a cake box and a container for crackers, etc.

The fireless cooker should be near the kitchen stove; and convenient storage place near at hand should be provided for the fireless cooker utensils when not in use.

We have outlined above a grouping that is based on the principle of conserving labor and energy, and that may be adapted to the needs of any kitchen no matter how faulty its construction. It requires comparatively small expense to make a kitchen convenient, in so far as convenience depends upon the proper arrangement and coördination of its portable equipment and supplies.

The processes analyzed thus far have been those that are carried on and completed in the kitchen. There are others which have to do with both kitchen and dining-room. Take for example those involving the use of supplies common to both kitchen and dining-room needs, like butter, milk, bread, crackers and drinking water. The best place for these is clearly the little pantry between the kitchen and dining-room, where they are equally accessible to both rooms. This end will be gained by placing the refrigerator, bread box, etc., in the pantry; and having near at hand the special utensils required for serving or handling these supplies.

After the cooking is done and the meal is ready to be served, we find that the table dishes divide themselves into three groups: First, those used to hold the cooked food; second, the dishes that must be warmed before they are ready for table use; and third, those that are used just as they are. While these groups are handled in three separate and distinct ways, they all belong to the same set of china. By the old method of grouping they would all be kept together in the dining-room closet. We shall now divide them so that they will be rightly grouped for their work. We take the platters, vegetable dishes and gravy boat to the kitchen closet; the plates, cups and saucers to a closet warmed by a coil from the furnace, so that they will be kept at the right temperature and ready for use at any time. We leave the third division in the dining-room closet, as near as possible to the linen supply and other table furnishings.

This scientific grouping has been tried out in a great number of cases and has been found wonderfully successful. By concentrating the working processes in one corner of the room, large kitchens have been made almost as convenient as small ones. Tiny rooms that did not seem large enough to be utilized for kitchen purposes have been made into most convenient kitchenettes. And awkward, badly planned kitchens have been transformed into efficient work rooms at small expense, just because working materials and utensils were grouped in a way that helped the work along instead of hindering and setting it back.

PRINCIPLES OF KITCHEN EFFICIENCY

As a means of putting into effect the principles of scientific grouping, it will be found very helpful to bear in mind the following general rules. They are based on the same idea of conserving time and strength, and thus enabling the worker to concentrate on constructive work all her best energy.

1. Keep nothing in the kitchen that is not used every day.
2. Things used oftenest should be most conveniently near at hand.
3. Grouping of utensils and supplies should be governed by the principle of Coördination of Processes.

Scientific grouping of equipment. Note service dishes in cupboard, bread-making outfit above refrigerator. Fireless-cooker on home-made stand beside wheel tray. Pastry table

4. Have narrow shelves with one row of things 🗸
on each.

5. Use open shelves rather than cupboards and
closed closets. (An exception to this rule
must be made where a coal range is used,
and the kitchen is necessarily dusty.)

6. Shelves should be at a convenient height, none
lower than 12 inches nor higher than can be
easily reached.

7. Nothing should be permitted to rest on the floor.
This saves bending over, and facilitates
cleaning the kitchen floor.

8. Have nothing in the kitchen that is not easy to
keep clean.

9. Fixed equipment should be placed where the
light is good.

10. Floor covering should be easy to keep clean and
pleasant for the feet to rest on.

11. Small utensils should be suspended from hooks 🗸
and cup-hooks fastened to the wall or the
edge of shelves.

12. Sink and work table should be at a convenient
height for the worker.

13. There should be a special place for each thing
used in the kitchen.

IV

BUILT-IN CONVENIENCES

EVERY kitchen ought to be so equipped with built-in conveniences that the portable equipment needed to make it a perfect work-room can be reduced to a minimum. In this book the term "Built-in Conveniences" means shelf-room and such other home-made contrivances as a carpenter can install.

While this problem has been well worked out in city apartments, and in country houses too, in certain sections of the country, as, for example, the perfectly equipped California bungalow, it is still unsolved in a large majority of cases. There are millions of kitchens in this country which could be transformed from awkward, inefficient work-rooms into convenient and well arranged work-rooms at comparatively small expense, by making a few vital alterations.

A family, on moving into a rented house, usually finds a stove, a sink and a china closet, nothing more. And the last is a purely accidental affair, contingent on the exigencies of architecture. Of a long list of built-in conveniences and fixed equipment which every home requires, these are the only needs

46

universally met, even in a primitive way. Yet these needs, one and all, are absolutely essential to comfort and efficiency, and could, with very slight expense, be made part of the original plan and structure of even the most modestly equipped kitchen.

Let us consider certain of these elementary needs which are common to all households, whether rich or poor, and see how they may be met, first in the building of new houses, second in transforming old ones.

NEEDS TO BE MET IN EVERY KITCHEN

1. Stove, sink and work-table.
2. Storage place for groceries.
3. Shelves, closet room or hooks for all kitchen utensils.
4. Refrigeration and cold storage for vegetables, fruit, etc.
5. Provision for keeping food warm.
6. Temporary receiving place for incoming supplies.
7. Place for cleaning outfit and cleaning preparations.
8. Closet for wraps near back entrance.
9. Box for coal or wood; shelf for kerosene or alcohol can.
10. Provision for disposing of kitchen waste.

Problems presented by the stove, sink, work-table and refrigerator will be considered elsewhere in this book, as will the very important subject of the disposing of kitchen waste. This chapter is concerned mainly with the storage problem, with *finding a place for things*. And this place must always be the most convenient and best possible, for the purpose of efficiency, of conserving the time and strength of the worker.

STORAGE PLACE FOR GROCERIES

In the old, haphazard kitchen planning, this need has usually been met by having one or more closets with end-shelves for the groceries. Sometimes this single closet or pantry must also hold many of the kitchen utensils. The shelves were usually wide, so that articles must be placed on them several layers deep. And the floor was used as a reserve shelf.

In other cases separate cupboards with wooden or glass doors were fastened to the kitchen wall, and designed to hold the cooking dishes, the larger closet being left entirely for supplies. In our trips about the country we find numbers of kitchens without any closet facilities whatever; many with only one closet; others with several. The location and number of closets, or the absence of them altogether has depended largely on how the outline of the kitchen lent itself to these requirements.

Approaching the matter from the new standpoint, that of creating an efficient work room, we realize at once that proper shelf-room, conveniently located, is one of the primary needs of the kitchen. We make that our starting-point and proceed to consider the resources and possibilities of the particular kitchen we are to build or reconstruct.

We find first of all that the wall space can be used to best advantage by having a system of narrow open shelves, rather than the deep-shelf closet or the cupboard with closed-in shelves and doors. We might have learned this long ago by noticing how much can be neatly and conveniently stored on open shelves in the grocery stores. Narrow shelves offer immense advantages over the deep-shelf plan. There is room for but one row of articles. Not having to reach behind the first row to get something at the back which, perhaps, we cannot see without standing on a chair, we are saved loss of time and energy due to awkward motions, and also the danger of knocking things off the shelf and breaking them. We find a further gain in doing away with doors and protecting the articles from dust by keeping them in carefully labeled glass or tin containers.

Finally, by the open-shelf system, we can have just the amount of shelf-room we require, no more and no less. And we can put the shelves where they are needed. This is the essential advantage of the open-shelf scheme, and is quite impossible in the case of closed-in cupboards, which must be put where there is room for them, and where the doors will not be in the way.

The most important supply shelves in the kitchen are those directly above the work table. The object is to have all needed supplies easily within reach of the worker's hand as she sits or stands at the work table. Here we see the importance of so locating doors and windows as to avoid breaking up the wall space. For the proper relation of work table to shelves is vital to our scheme of efficiency, and should be worked out in the original planning of the kitchen.

Sometimes it is possible, instead of a portable work-table to have a broad work-shelf built-in, across the entire width of the kitchen. Such a work-shelf is an ideal convenience. The dimensions should be 22 inches wide, and a height to suit the worker. A good average height is 32 inches, over all, from the floor. It may be covered with zinc for a small additional cost. ($1.75 for the zinc, about six feet long.)

For the supply shelves the following dimensions will be found convenient. Have the lowest one 6 inches wide to hold supplies kept in glass fruit jars or tutti-frutti jars. This shelf should be 15½ inches above the work table, or 47½ inches above the floor. Two four-inch wide shelves may be placed above this, making them 7½ inches apart. In some cases it is possible to have the shelves extend around one or both ends of the work table, as well as across the width of it.

The space under the work-table or work-shelf may be utilized partly for drawers, and partly for broad shelves to hold some of the bulkier parts of the kitchen equipment. The drawers may be used, one for cutlery, the other for kitchen towels. Additional space, when there is plenty, as in the case of a long, built-in work-shelf, may be closed in and converted into flour bins and additional drawers. This gives immense storage capacity to even a little kitchenette 7 feet by 11. The shelves above such a work-table will hold the full list of groceries enumerated on pages 209 and 210, which represents the normal and well-chosen supply that a family of five needs to carry in stock. The drawers below, if adapted in size to the requirements of the rest of the kitchen will make a butler's pantry unnecessary.

PLACES FOR KITCHEN UTENSILS

The open-shelf system has the same advantages for storing the kitchen utensils as it has for the storage of groceries. It enables us to keep the equipment within easy reach of the place where it is to be used. Shelves above the sink provide a convenient place for pitchers, measuring cups, coffee and tea outfits, egg beater and strainers; also for the sink solutions used in cleaning. Stew pans and various small utensils may be suspended by means of cup-hooks from the wall back of the sink, from the edge of the shelf, or under the shelf.

The best width for the shelf to hold sink solutions is 4 inches. A good height is 56 inches from the floor. The shelf for pitchers should be 6 inches wide.

For bread and cake mixers and other equipment of an awkward size special shelves must be provided wherever there is space enough, or where nooks and corners of the room can be utilized to advantage. These should be the proper size to hold the equipment which is designed to rest on them. They should not be lower than the knee or inconveniently high, as we must avoid the awkward motions of bending over and reaching up.

Some housekeepers like to keep nearly all the equipment on shelves, while others prefer to hang everything from the wall that can be hung, leaving the shelf-room for supplies and equipment without handles. The latter is really the best arrangement for most kitchens, although very convenient kitchenettes are planned in the former way. (See illustration facing page 94.)

In old kitchens where ample closet room has been provided for groceries and supplies, it is still convenient to have at least two shelves put up in the kitchen; one 6 inches wide above the sink, and one 4 inches wide above the work table. This will provide a place for the small supplies most constantly used in mixing and baking.

The closet will then have to be studied most carefully, and its wall space arranged to the best advantage. By experiment we found that 4 feet square was a most convenient size for a provision closet. In a closet of this size one could stand in the center and reach without stretching everything

that was at the end or sides. The top shelf should
be 5 feet from the floor and 6 inches wide, and
should extend around all three sides. Below this
on the right hand side should be three shelves, the
lowest 14 inches from the floor and 12 inches wide,
to hold the week's supply of potatoes, apples, etc.
This shelf will need at least 18 inches " head-room,"
so that a peach basket containing vegetables may
stand on it. The other two shelves should be 6
inches wide and about one foot apart.

At the end of such a closet it is convenient to
have a small table with an under shelf and a drawer.
Just back of the table should be three shelves against
the wall, the lowest 12 inches wide to hold the
larger kitchen utensils; the other two, each 6 inches
wide. Most of the wall space on the left hand side
of the closet is left free for hooks. On these may
be hung the griddle, muffin tins, meat grinder,
chopping bowl, etc., things not in constant use, and
which, therefore, need not take up valuable kitchen
wall space.

The best hooks to use for suspending articles from
the wall, we found to be the square cup-hooks with
shank an inch long. The three-quarter inch round
cub-hooks are the best for the smaller articles.

COLD STORAGE FACILITIES

Very many housekeepers do not realize that they
could get along without ice for eight or nine months
of the year if they had a good cold closet, built into

an outer wall of the kitchen, and properly ventilated. (See Fig. 4.)   If the house is a new one the cold closet should be provided for in the original plan of the house.   Convenient dimensions are the follow-

FIG. 4.—Sketch of cold closet. Dimensions: 2 feet wide, 2 feet 10½ inches high, 19 inches deep.

ing: Let the closet be 24 inches wide, 34½ inches high and 19 inches deep.   Fit it up with three shelves the full depth of the closet.   Let the first shelf be 11 inches above the closet floor; the next 7¾ inches above that; and the third 7¾ inches above the second.   The cold closet is really a box set against the outer wall of the kitchen, and with an opening into the kitchen exactly like a window casing.   It extends through and a little beyond the outer wall, and has a sloping top to shed the rain. A door is made to fit the opening into the kitchen.

Holes for ventilation are bored through the lower shelves and at the top of the outside wall, and these are protected by screen cloth.   The closet may have double walls, insulated as a home-made ice chest is; but it is usually a simple box with wooden walls.

This size will hold everything necessary for a family of five; but a slightly larger closet would be more convenient.   An ideal size is 4 feet wide, 5 feet 6 inches high, and 22 inches deep.   This will provide space for four shelves placed a foot apart. The two upper shelves should be the full depth of the closet, and the lower two, half the depth.

The best location for such a closet is in the kitchen shed or vestibule.   It ought to have two doors opening toward the center, or it may be covered by a window shade.   The north exposure is the coolest location.

In rented houses a perfectly satisfactory cold closet may be made by taking out a window sash (if the window is not needed for light), and making the box extension on the outside a little larger than the opening.   Or simply the lower half of the window may be thus utilized.   The sash is then left in place, and raising the window gives access to the closet.   By this arrangement the light from the upper half of the window is still available.

THE BEST COLD CLOSET OF ALL

There is no reason why every country house should not have the most perfect of all cold storage rooms in the cellar underneath the kitchen, and connected with the kitchen by means of a dumb-waiter located in an air shaft. The dumb-waiter could have two or three shelves to hold the small supplies that are usually kept in the refrigerator; and one wide, deep shelf to use in sending up apples, potatoes and winter vegetables, that could be purchased in quantity. Such a cellar should be made by excavating below the main cellar. Its walls and sides should be concreted. Good ventilation should be insured by a properly constructed air shaft. It would be better to depend on artificial light, as it will be a better storage place if kept dark.

With such a cold storage place every family could buy supplies in quantity, could put down eggs for winter use, could keep extra vegetables grown in the home garden; and could be independent of the ice-man the year round. Such a convenience would tend to restore to the home some of its lost independence. Of course it would require work and vigilance to take care of the supplies, and above all to care for a garden. But it is work that the average man, spending too many hours over a desk, really needs to keep him in health. The care of practical home interests is a great restorative force, and builds up the sense of independence which modern business conditions seem destined entirely to destroy.

KEEPING FOOD WARM

This problem is so important to the efficiency of the kitchen that it will be dealt with in another chapter. It must be thought out when the heating system is planned, and can be very easily solved if provision is made for it at the time of building the house, or in connection with installing the heating system.

CARE OF INCOMING SUPPLIES

Hours of needless interruption can be saved by providing a safe and still, a compact wooden closet, fastened to the wall of the back entrance porch. It should have a screen door equipped with a spring catch, and two shelves about 10 inches wide. The lower of these shelves should be 10 inches above the floor of the closet, since a milk bottle is 9½ inches high. The second may be 8 inches above that, and 8 inches from the top of the closet.

In cases where there is a very small entrance porch, or none at all, a window-seat box with hinged top may be placed in the kitchen porch to answer the same purpose. A zinc lining will protect either closet or box from insects.

We have made it a policy for nine years to cut out the useless waste of time due to continual interruption by the delivery-man. We have tried the plan in city homes as well as in the country, and have found it to work admirably. We have it understood when we give orders that if anything sent to us is not satisfactory, we will return it. We check up the slips carefully before we put the food away, and telephone at once if anything is wrong so that the trouble may be rectified. We make a note on the slip and keep it on our desk until the matter has been adjusted. We pay for honest, efficient service, and demand it. On our side we are considerate about not requiring unnecessary deliveries, and we pay our bills promptly. We have never met with any loss from this policy. It takes the merchant only two or three lessons to learn that if orders are wrong they will have to be called for and made right. And mistress and maid alike are saved hours of unnecessary interruption.

CLOSET FOR CLEANING OUTFIT

The kitchen cleaning outfit usually includes all the implements, cloths and materials for cleaning the lower floor of the house, and the size of the outfit depends on the general style of the house, how much woodwork or brass there is, and other details of finish. In large houses there should be a closet on every floor large enough to hold everything that is needed to do this work to best advantage. (See Fig. 5.)

The chemicals used for cleaning should be kept in glass jars, carefully labeled. The cloths may be folded up in a tin box, or hung from hooks by means of loops. The mops, brooms, brushes, etc., should have screw-eyes fastened to the ends and should always be hung up when not in use. There should be a reserve supply of cleaning cloths kept in a drawer near the closet, or in a box on the shelf. Old stew-pans, tins, etc., needed for mixing the

FIG. 5.— Sketch of convenient closet for cleaning outfit. Dimensions: 3 to 4 feet wide, 6 feet 6 inches high, 12 to 18 inches deep. Shelf 12 inches wide and 10 inches from top of closet.

cleaning preparations, should be kept near at hand on a shelf.

For a full list of desirable equipment for cleaning see page 180, Chapter XIII on Daily care of the Kitchen.

In order to hang up the long-handled mops and allow for a shelf above, the closet should be 6 feet 6 inches high. It may be 12 to 18 inches deep, and 3 to 4 feet wide. It will be more convenient to have two doors opening in the middle; but one will be less expensive, and also sufficient if the closet

is not more than three feet wide. The cleat from
which to hang the long-handled mops should be 5
feet 3 inches from the floor.   The closet floor should
be 2 inches above the floor of the room, and should
be covered with oilcloth, so it will be easy to keep
clean.   The shelf should be 12 inches wide and 10
inches from the top of the closet.   Such a closet will
be found a wonderful comfort in any home.   It
can very easily and economically be made by a carpenter.   Or a metamorphosed old wardrobe will
answer the purpose very well.

Where it is not possible to have a special
closet for the cleaning things, they may be cared for
as follows: For the brooms, mops, etc., have a
cleat three inches wide nailed to the wall 5 feet 5
inches above the floor.   Hooks are screwed into this
cleat, and here the long-handled mops and brooms
may be hung.   The wall back of the landing to the
cellar may be fitted up in this way.   A special cleat
3 feet high and more conveniently located, should be
provided for the dust pan and brush.   As these implements are in constant use, they ought to be readily
at hand.   The rest of the cleaning outfit may be
kept in drawers or on a shelf in another closet.
They ought to be kept out of the way of the children, as none of these chemicals can be recommended as desirable playthings for the little people.

The importance of having a generous supply of
fresh cleaning cloths cannot be too strongly empha-
sized.   More time is lost " hunting up cloths " than

any housekeeper realizes. By fitting out generously with cleaning cloths and then insisting on having the ones in use kept clean, this need can be met with very little expense, and a great saving of time.

CLOSET FOR WRAPS AT BACK ENTRANCE

Every family needs a closet for every-day wraps; but where there are little children this need is imperative. If a closet near the rear entrance is fitted up especially for the children, with a coat-bar and hooks the right height for them, they can soon be taught to place their coats on coat-bars, hang up their hats and place their rubbers on the special shelf made for overshoes near the bottom of the closet. All tracking through the house with wet and dirty clothes in search of Mama, may then be saved. What this means in economy of time and strength cannot be estimated where the cleaning-up falls on a maid. Where the mother herself does the work she soon finds what a large item it amounts to. Children cannot be taught to hang up their things unless given suitable conveniences for this. For children under twelve the hooks should be about three feet from the floor.

The space above the hooks and coat-bar may be reserved for shelves. The lowest of these may be used for the children's hats. The others for any household need not otherwise met. Among these may be mentioned the small outfit of tools that every housekeeper should have,

The coat closet may be 6 feet 4½ inches high; 18 inches deep and 3 feet 2½ inches wide. The floor may be 1½ inches above the main floor, and should be covered with oil-cloth. The children's coat-bar, as has been said, should be 3 feet from the floor. The space above the coat-bar may be conveniently divided into three shelves placed 9½ inches apart. The lower shelf, for hats, should be 12 inches wide; and the two upper ones 8 inches wide.

If it is impossible to have more than one closet for wraps, it ought to be made four feet wide, with room at the side to hang up the every-day wraps of the grown-ups. Or a cleat may be fastened to the wall in the back entrance hall to answer this need. But whether or not the convenience of the grown-ups can be considered in this particular, it is a necessity, wherever there are children, to have a special closet for their use with hooks and coat-bar the right height.

A PLACE FOR THE KITCHEN FUELS

Wherever a wood or coal stove is in use in the kitchen, there ought to be a place near the stove for a small reserve of fuel. This is usually provided for in the case of wood stoves; but very often no provision is made for lightening the labor of carrying coal. If it is not desirable to have a coal box, there should be two separate coal hods, so that one may always be in reserve, making it unnecessary to go to the coal bin more than once a day.

Very ingenious devices are found in country homes for so locating the coal bin that the supply is near at hand. In some cases an inexpensive dumb-waiter has been installed, on which coal may be brought up from the cellar.

With the widespread use of kerosene and alcohol as fuels, it is important to suggest here the advantage of having a wide shelf, zinc-covered, on which the large supply-can may rest. The best cans have funnel arrangements for use when filling the small can. The supply-can must be kept in a safe place. The shelf should be about 12 inches wide and 2 feet from the floor. Kerosene cans and alcohol cans should never be kept on the same shelf. It is very easy to pick up the wrong can and fill the kerosene lamp with alcohol, or the alcohol stove with kerosene. The results, it is needless to state, are discouraging.

V

Heating the Kitchen and Keeping Dishes Warm

IN very many cases the first step toward creating an efficient kitchen is banishing the coal stove. The choice of fuels will be dealt with in a subsequent chapter. But just here we must consider certain needs which immediately arise when the coal stove is discarded, and which are closely related to the structural problems of building or remodeling the work-room. These needs are heating the kitchen and keeping the food warm after it is cooked, until it is ready to be served.

In the days when fuel was not the expensive item that it is to-day, one of the great advantages of the wood or coal range was that it heated the kitchen besides doing the cooking. In small houses it also did practically all the heating of the house, except for four or five months of intensely cold weather. The pipe from the kitchen stove went up through the ceiling and heated the chamber above. The door from the kitchen to the dining-room was left open, so that the heat might pass through and make the latter room comfortable. A fireplace, in addition, in two or three rooms, or a coal stove or two, kept the house at a fair temperature even in very cold weather. Under such conditions a wood stove or coal range in the kitchen is still to be recommended. But where the rest of the house is equipped with a good heating system there is no reason why the kitchen should not be included in the general heating plan. This eliminates the necessity of cooking by coal in hot weather, when the heat of a coal range is an added affliction to the cook; it takes from the kitchen all the burden of dust and ashes; and it adds very little in the way of extra fuel to the expense of running the furnace.

All persons who keep domestic help know that the coal range is very wastefully run. They also know that it requires the best grade of intelligence to run a coal range economically and get results. As very few mistresses understand the matter themselves, and the few that do cannot get maids who are willing to be trained in matters of economy, the result is that the coal stove is no longer an economy and can only hold its place on the ground that it does its work more satisfactorily than any other fuel. This is no longer found to be the case. Gas stoves, kerosene stoves and alcohol stoves are all found to be easier to take care of and less expensive to operate than the coal range except in the case of very large families or where a large amount of baking is done.

The necessity thus arises for heating the kitchen

independently of the cook stove. To extend the furnace heat to the kitchen and provide a hot-air register or radiator costs from $15 to $25. This is a very simple matter in the case of a new house. But in houses where the furnace is already installed there is not always enough heating capacity to heat an extra room. In the West very few gas kitchens are heated at all. And, indeed, this is far from being a serious hardship in a house which is otherwise well heated. The kitchen is no longer regarded as a sitting-room for the family or the maid. One is always briskly working. In fact, unless the kitchen is in a cold location or the furnace does not adequately heat the rest of the house, it is often safe to ignore this problem. In a case where the kitchen must be heated and the furnace will not do it, the coal range should always be retained. A supplementary gas, alcohol or kerosene stove may be used for emergencies and summer cooking.

There are a number of good portable heaters on the market burning kerosene or gas, and these are useful for supplementing the furnace heat in any room. But as they quickly deprive the air of oxygen, a room in which they are used should be well aired from time to time.

PROVISION FOR KEEPING FOOD AND DISHES WARM

Of equal importance to the heating of the kitchen is the problem of keeping food warm and warming dishes that are to be used on the table. This is a very simple matter in a coal kitchen. The best coal ranges are equipped with good warming shelves. Where the warming shelves are not provided, as in the case of a cheaper range, it is possible to have a tinsmith make a serviceable substitute of Japanned iron, which can be placed above the stove at a convenient height. These iron shelves should have round holes cut through for ventilation, and may be supported against the wall by means of brackets.

In a gas kitchen this matter of warming-shelves presents much greater difficulty and requires more thought. With the gas stove we have no longer a constant radiation of warm air which can be utilized not only for the purposes named above, but for raising bread and drying the kitchen-ware. These needs must now be provided for in some other way.

The larger gas ranges have a warming oven above the elevated baking oven, which is kept hot by the oven burner when the latter is in use. At other times the warming oven may be heated by lighting the pilot burner. In gas ranges having two baking ovens, one is always available for a warming oven by using the pilot burner. Even with these facilities it is a great advantage to have some kind of supplementary warming appliance. In kitchens heated by steam or hot water this is easily managed by purchasing flat-topped grills to fit over the kitchen radiator. These grills come in different sizes and may be painted the color of the radiator. With these the heat of the radiator is always available to dry kitchen towels, pots and pans and

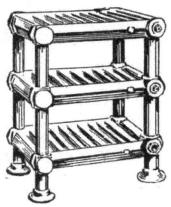

FIG. 6.— Pantry radiators like the above are fairly reasonable in price and valuable for keeping dishes warm.

the like. Both dining-room and kitchen radiators may be thus equipped. The grills cost from $1.25 to $1.50, according to size. The dining-room radiator grill is very convenient ·for warming dishes that do not need to go to the kitchen at all.

In homes where it is possible to have special warming facilities in the pantry the closet where the table service is kept may be warmed by having heating coils pass under the shelves. In other cases special pantry radiators (Fig. 6) are manufactured which have two shelves made of coils heated from the furnace.

In even the simplest home, this need may be met

by having a shelf built back of the three-burner Junior gas stove in the kitchen.   In such a case the gas stove should be set out a little from the wall. The shelf may be made the same height and covered with zinc.   A portable oven may be heated on a regular gas burner and then set back on this shelf to serve as a warming closet for the dishes. In such a case it is well to have in addition a two or four shelf steamer in which food may be placed in the serving dishes and kept hot until it is ready to be put on the table.

VI

Hot Water Heating Systems

AN abundant supply of hot water for the kitchen and bathroom can be obtained at very moderate maintenance cost if one knows just the best equipment to select. Enough money is spent in equipping and running the average home to insure this comfort. But, strangely enough, it is the exception and not the rule to find the hot water situation really successfully handled.

Some systems give good results when properly installed, but prove very inadequate when the installation is faulty. Of such are the various methods of " heating by waste heat." Another prolific cause of disappointment is the installation of apparatus which turns out to be very expensive to maintain. This type gives good results, but cannot be used freely because of the mammoth size of the monthly bills resulting from anything like a liberal use of hot water. This condition of affairs is pitiable when we realize that the amount of money actually spent, if wisely spent, would have secured abundance! If one must always be worrying about hot water, why not go back to the old-fashioned range, with the water-box in the end?

This type gives very good service and enough hot water for the needs of careful people. You never expect to have an abundant supply of hot water for kitchen or bathroom unless you exercise a certain amount of forethought. Consequently you plan ahead, whereas, with a hot-water system that is supposed to work but does not, you are continually disappointed and are grieved to find the same old difficulty arising day after day. It requires great moral courage to consider your investment a total failure and have it taken out. But if you have made a bad selection this course is the only satisfactory one in the end.

HEATING BY "WASTE HEAT"

Two systems of hot-water heating in very general use are based on utilizing the so-called "waste heat" of the furnace or the kitchen range. These are satisfactory under favorable conditions and when well installed. But equipment based on a better principle is now on the market, and ultimately will replace these types. As few housekeepers, however, are in a position to choose new hot-water heating apparatus, we shall first consider the problem of getting good results from the systems in common use.

For many years the hot-water supply of the average home has been heated by means of coils placed in the fire box of the kitchen range, or by an iron water-back furnished with the range. The water-back is the one in common use. The success of this method has depended on the size and construction of the range, its efficient management, and the size of the boiler so connected. Where the boiler is too large for the heating capacity of the range, a supply of lukewarm water is the result. For this there is no remedy but installing a smaller boiler or a larger range. In families where the range must be run economically, the amount of fuel necessary for cooking alone proves insufficient for giving a satisfactory supply of hot water. In at least eighty per cent of our homes the coal range is run at an extravagant waste of fuel, as far as the requirements of cooking alone are concerned. This is getting to be a serious matter, now that coal is growing more expensive every year. The truth is that the water is not warmed by waste heat, but by *wasted* heat — heat that need not be wasted if the range were not expected to heat the water in addition to cooking the food. Ranges without water backs can be run on less than half a ton of coal a month, and will do a great deal of cooking under skilful management. One experienced housekeeper was able to effect this result using *pea coal* as fuel. It could not be said that she accomplished this result by stinting her family (of five people!), as she was the champion cook of the neighborhood. Where this system is already installed, it will be made more effective and economical by jacketing the boiler (*i. e.,* covering the boiler with some thick substance to prevent radiation and conserve the heat). (See Fig. 8.)

Another system based on the idea of conserving waste heat makes use of the furnace to heat the water supply during the winter months. Heating coils are placed in the fire-box of the furnace, and the water system is connected with these. This system is used extensively in private homes, and the result is in many cases very satisfactory. Here too, however, the hot water heating is done not by " waste heat," but by wasted heat; heat that would not be required for the ordinary purposes of the furnace. Unfortunately it is impossible to estimate just how much the hot water heating system takes away from the efficiency of the furnace, or adds to the operating cost. Heating contractors tell us that they have to make a liberal extra allowance for houses where heating coils are to be used, as there is no way of judging how much of the heat will be diverted by the needs of the water heating system. Many heating contractors do not recommend this system on that account. It does not work at all where cheaply constructed furnaces are used. Under favorable conditions it gives very satisfactory results.

In very many localities lime deposits in the water settle in the pipes of the coil, and it is necessary to take them out at intervals and have them cleansed or replaced. The cost is about the same in either case, so it is usually best to put in new ones. The expense is between six and ten dollars, and may have to be met every year or every two years, according to the locality.

INDEPENDENT HOT WATER HEATING SYSTEMS

Families who really want to apply the principles of Scientific Management in their homes, are advised to select a water heating system that is independent of both the range and the furnace. It will then be possible to keep accurate records of fuel expense. These records will be of immense value to the housekeeper in economically managing her own household, and will be of equal value to other housekeepers. When it is realized in private homes that intelligent study of the operating expense will result in more comfortable and more economical living, we shall begin to develop a real science of house management.

One of the simplest and most efficient methods of heating water independently of the range and furnace is by the use of small coal stoves especially constructed for the purpose. They are called " Hot Water or Laundry Heaters," and are connected to the kitchen range boiler. (See Fig. 7.) They are made in different sizes, adapted to different boiler capacities, and have either cast iron or brass water pots. The cast iron is less expensive than the brass and can be used in localities where the water is free from substances that act on iron. This system is most efficient when the boiler is enclosed in an asbestos jacket to prevent radiation and conserve the heat of the water. Canvas covered jackets lined with asbestos are now on the market, made

FIG. 7.— Small laundry heater with iron or brass water pot, connected with boiler in cellar.

in various sizes to fit different boilers. It is also advisable to have the fire pot of the heater covered with plastic asbestos.

In bungalows or very simple country homes this little heater can be made to serve a double use by encasing the smoke-pipe and the stove and delivering the warm air to a room on the second or third floor. The house at Darien which served as the first Experiment Station, had a bathroom so heated. The lower floor only was heated by the house furnace, which consequently was operated at a minimum expense of time and fuel.

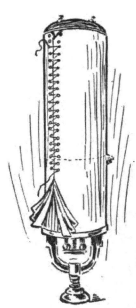

FIG. 8.— Canvas jackets lined with asbestos are now on the market made to fit any boiler.

This type of hot-water heater has two advantages over the other types. It keeps the cellar free from all dampness in the summer-time, warming the floors above it at the same time. It also acts as a supplementary stove, where vegetables with a strong odor may be cooked. In many small houses where the kitchen is not well ventilated these odors pass from the kitchen to the dining-room and often to other rooms, so it is found to be a great advantage to have all cooking of this kind done in the basement.

The cost of the system, using the smallest type of laundry heater and a forty-gallon galvanized iron boiler, is about twenty-eight dollars, including installation. A jacket (see Fig. 8) will cost three dollars and a half more, making the total cost thirty-one dollars and a half. This size will furnish an abundant supply of hot water for a family of five, and can be operated at an average cost of one dollar and a half per month, if pea coal is used for fuel. With expert management in small families the cost need not exceed seventy-five cents a month. This cost also covers its use for laundry purposes. This type of heater, in larger sizes, has been successfully installed in houses having several bathrooms, and has given good results in apartment houses.

In tests by Mr. Charles Barnard at the Experiment Station, the following record was made showing the operating cost of the small heater for a family of two. These tests also showed the efficiency of the jacket in conserving heat, and in maintaining the temperature of the water after it had been heated.

MR, BARNARD'S TEST OF HOT WATER HEATER

After a few preliminary trials to ascertain the fuel capacity of the heater, the following records were made:

First day, 8.00 A. M. Fire started. Temperature of water in the boiler, 79 Fahr.; 8.53 A. M., fire checked; 9.30, temperature of water 90; at 10.30, temperature 106; 2 P. M., fire out; 6:30 P. M., temperature of water 90. Coal burned, 7 pounds.

Second day, 9.15 A. M. Started fire; water temperature 82; 2.45 P. M., good fire burning; temperature of water 130. 4.30 P. M., fire out; water temperature 130. Coal burned, 7 pounds. Other days gave same results.

These results were very satisfactory. A great deal of hot water was used every day in the kitchen and more or less used every day in the bath room. The amount of coal burned was 7 pounds each twenty-four hours. The water during the day was hot enough for all purposes and often too hot to touch. The fire burned on an average six hours out of twenty-four. To secure still greater economy of heat it was decided to conserve the heat in the boiler by clothing the boiler with a canvas jacket lined with asbestos. Such a jacket was drawn over the boiler and laced together; the temperature of the room being 76, and the water 103.

At 7 A. M. the next morning the fire was started and at 7.30 the fire was checked. At 9 A. M. the water temperature was 122; at 10.30 A. M., 136; at 2.30 P. M., 136; at 8.00 P. M., 122. During the entire day the room temperature remained almost stationary, rising only two degrees in the afternoon.

The next morning the water temperature was 100, showing a loss in twelve hours with no fire, of only 22 degrees. This conservation of heat showed the efficiency of the jacket on the boiler. It should also be observed that the rise in the temperature during the previous day was greater than before the jacket was put on, the rise between 7.30 and 10.30 being 37 degrees. The following day was very warm. With all the windows open the temperature of the room rose slowly from 73 to 79. Between 8.00 A. M., when the fire was started, and noon, the temperature of the water rose 42 degrees, and at 9 P. M. was 130, the fire being out.

Next morning the room temperature was 72 and the water 108, a loss of heat of only 22 degrees in nine hours. The fire was started at 10 A. M., and in two hours the temperature of the water was 130. At 4 P. M. the fire was out, and at 8 P. M. the water had lost only 4 degrees.

Next morning no fire, and at 8 A. M. the water in the boiler was 104, showing a loss of heat of 22 degrees in 12 hours. At noon the water was 98, showing a total loss of 32 degrees only in 20 hours. At 1.00 P. M. the fire was started and at 8.00 P. M. had gone out, the water at 9.00 P. M. being 145. At 7.00 A. M. next day the temperature of the water was 118, and at 1.00 P. M., 100. Other trials showed that if the fire burned six hours, the water would be hot enough for washing the dishes twenty-four hours after the fire had gone out.

A study of these and many other records showed that this simple and comparatively inexpensive method of supplying hot water in a country house is both efficient and economic. On one day the amount of coal burned was five pounds; on another day, eight pounds, the average consumption being seven pounds a day. The fire burned about six hours each day; for, so great was the economy of heat gained by jacketing the boiler that heat once stored in the boiler was sufficient for dish washing for twenty-four hours. It was found best to allow the fire to die out after once heating the water in the boiler, because a continuous fire would supply more hot water than could be used in the ordinary work of the house. . . .

From a careful estimate of the amount of hot water required for a family of five, it is believed that such an installation would supply all the hot water needed at an average fuel consumption of not more than fifteen pounds of nut coal a day.

Such a system as this will give an ample supply of hot water for the kitchen and one bathroom. Where a larger supply is needed, it may be secured by using a larger sized boiler and heater.

LOCATION AND CARE OF THE HOT WATER HEATER

The cellar is, in most houses, the most convenient place for the heater. The boiler may be placed in the kitchen in horizontal or vertical position, or it may be placed in the cellar near the heater. Under ordinary conditions the latter location is recommended because it saves valuable kitchen space. When the boiler must be placed in the kitchen, the jacket may be painted to match the kitchen walls.

During the months when the furnace is in use it will require but very little extra care to run the hot-water heater. Several very efficient makes are on the market which are exceedingly simple to run, requiring less care than an ordinary kitchen range, and much less intelligence. Pea coal, one of the cheapest sizes of hard coal, gives excellent results.

HOT WATER BY MEANS OF GAS HEATERS

There are four types of gas heaters on the market, and several different makes of each type.

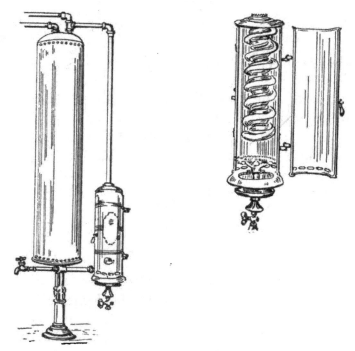

FIG. 9.—Represents the type of gas heater with coils outside the boiler. The drawing at the right shows a view of the coils when door of drum is open. The figure at the left shows the heater as it looks when installed in any kitchen.

Whichever type is selected, it is very important to select the heater which is best of its kind.

The earlier types of gas heater are operated on the principle of water circulating in heating coils placed outside the boiler. (See Fig. 9.) While they satisfactorily do the work of heating the water, there is great loss of fuel efficiency due to radiation. Much of the heat of the water in the coils is given up

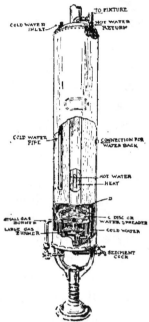

FIG. 10.—Illustrates one of the simplest types of hot water boiler with gas heater enclosed within boiler. The large gas burner is located in the lower part of the boiler. It is lighted by the small gas burner. Cold water enters the boiler through the cold water inlet. The water to be heated enters the pipe at D, passes down and up through the centre of the large burner into disc or water spreader marked C. Then passes up through the flue to the T at the top of the boiler. The T connects in one direction with the boiler itself and in the other with the hot water faucets. The hot water being heated within the boiler instead of outside as shown in Fig. 9, is protected from loss of heat by radiation.

to warm the air of the kitchen. In the cheaper heaters of this type where the coils are of iron instead of brass, the loss due to rapid cooling is a very important item. This difficulty can be partially overcome by jacketing the boiler.

COMBINATION BOILER AND HEATER

Special kitchen boilers are now constructed having the burners enclosed in the lower end of the boiler itself. (See Fig. 10.) The heating pipe passes up through a cylindrical air chamber in the center of the boiler. There is no loss of heat by radiation, either from the heating compartment or the hot water pipe, as these are in contact with the inner walls of the boiler, and not with the outer air. Within a few moments of the time when the burner is lighted hot water is ready to be drawn off.

The best makes are of heavy galvanized iron or copper, with wooden insulating walls. If not made with an insulating covering of some kind, it is wise to encase the outer walls of the boiler with an asbestos jacket. These are made to fit any size of boiler, and cost $3.50. Boilers of this type cost from $30.00 to $65.00, according to size and make. They may be connected to the water back of the ordinary coal range, or to the heating coils of the furnace. They are therefore available in every home.

GAS HEATER PLACED UNDER THE KITCHEN BOILER

Another very simple and efficient gas water heater is now on the market which heats the water inexpensively by direct contact heat. It consists of a cast iron plate with sixteen annular air spaces through which the gas is delivered, and operates on the principle of the Argand burner or central draft burner. The casting may be clamped under any kitchen boiler and is very inexpensive to connect. It is connected with the main gas supply by means of two mixing burners so that the gas is mixed with the proper amount of air and produces a very intense flame. The sixteen little openings of the casting are supplied with this gas. As the heat is most intense at the tip of the flame it is important to have the casting placed at the right distance under the boiler. If it is placed too close the flame is spread, and what is known as a " floating flame " is produced. This kind of flame does not give the same degree of heat.

This little appliance costs $6.50 and can be connected to any boiler for from $2.50 to $4.00, the price depending on the plumber who does the work. It also connects with a thermostat arrangement which adds to the expense. The manufacturer's tests state that the contents of a thirty-six gallon boiler can be heated in summer time to a scalding point at a cost of two cents, and that the same temperature may be maintained for ten hours for six cents. This cost may be further reduced by jacketing the boiler with corrugated asbestos to conserve the heat.

"INSTANTANEOUS" WATER HEATERS

Two well known and well developed systems of "instantaneous" water heating are on the market and are generally recommended by architects for large and small houses where economy is not a seriously important consideration. The "instantaneous" heater, which is somewhat like a stove in appearance, is equipped with five sections of copper heating coils. As soon as a hot water faucet is turned on, an automatic valve lights the powerful gas burners in the heater and the hot water is forced to the open faucet. When the faucet is turned off the valve closes and the flame is extinguished.

These heaters are equipped with temperature thermometers which automatically maintain a safe and desirable water temperature. They are often installed for summer in houses where the water is heated in winter by coils in the furnace. These are very convenient and desirable, but must, for the present at least, be regarded as luxuries within the reach of only prosperous families. They are expensive in operating cost, and expensive in repairs. This, added to the first cost of $85 to $160, not counting installation, makes them prohibitive for families having an income of less than $5,000.

This conclusion has not been arrived at from tests at the Experiment Station, but from a careful consideration of the principles of construction and of the facts presented by housekeepers who have had practical experience with this type of heater.

As regards the reliability of the manufacturers and the matter of good construction, we have no hesitation in stating that these systems do the work they are said to do. The facts not explained by the manufacturers or by agents are: the wastefulness of the principle in places where a constant supply of hot water is not needed, as in a private home. To produce quick results an extravagant degree of heat is required for a few moments only. Furthermore, in case of needed repairs, the complexity of construction makes it an expensive matter to renew the parts.

KEROSENE WATER HEATERS

A convenient little heater made on the principle of the blue-flame kerosene stove is now on the market, and does very satisfactory work. It is constructed with copper coils *outside* the boiler. As we have already explained, the defect of this system is loss of heat through radiation. By jacketing the boiler the heat of the water can be conserved. In a two-months' test at the author's summer home, we found that it took two hours to heat a forty-gallon boiler, and that the cost, with kerosene at fifteen cents a gallon, was a little over two cents an hour.

When it comes to quoting the cost of any plumbing fixtures or apparatus and giving the cost of installation, only approximate figures can be given. The manufacturers sell only to their agents and allow a very wide margin between the quoted price and the price at which the fixtures may actually be sold. Then again plumbers have to supply fittings and time that vary widely according to the location of each appliance. So it is always necessary to get accurate quotations of a local plumber of just what it will cost in a given case. It is a help, however, to have a general idea of what each different system of hot water heating will cost under average conditions, and the figures given here have been learned from actual experience and checked up by figures given by contractors in this vicinity.

Cost of equipment where coal range is used:

Water-back connection to kitchen range .... $ 5.00
Heavy galvanized iron boiler, thirty gallons 10.00
Cost of installation, $5 to $8; usual price 5.00
Jacket for boiler 3.50
                                              _____
                                               $23.50

Cost of laundry stove gas heater with coils outside or blue-flame kerosene heater:

Average price, best grade of each, $12 to $15.... $12.00
Heavy galvanized iron boiler, thirty gallons 10.00
Average cost of installation 6.00
Jacket for boiler 3.50
                                              _____
                                               $31.50

Cost of gas heaters of other types:

Cost of gas heater placed under kitchen boiler .... $ 6.50
Heavy galvanized iron boiler, thirty gallons 10.00
Cost of installation, $2.50 to $4; average price.... 3.25
Jacket for boiler 3.50
                                              _____
                                               $23.25

Cost of gas heater with coil inside boiler ....$ 30.00
Cost of installation 5.00

$35.00

Cost of same with thermostat connection ......$ 65.00

Cost of instantaneous heaters (gas) from $85 to
$160; average ....$ 85.00
Cost of installation 28.00

$113.00

VII

CHOICE OF FUEL FOR COOKING

THERE are six safe fuels for kitchen use: wood, coal, gas, kerosene, denatured alcohol and electricity. Cooking appliances have been so perfected that any one of these may be used to meet the needs of the household. The choice is largely a matter of expediency and cost.

WOOD

Wood was the first fuel to be used, and is still in general use in farming communities where each family has a wood lot, and can obtain its supply at small expense. It is a very satisfactory fuel under right conditions, and does not require the skill and forethought necessary to successfully manage a coal range. It cannot furnish sustained heat and is therefore practicable only in kitchens where there is no modern plumbing or where a separate heater is installed to heat the water supply. The chief annoyance connected with its use is that it blackens the bottom of the cooking utensils. The most serious disadvantage of cooking with wood has been overcome by the perfecting of the fireless cooker. Any long process like baking or steaming used to be very troublesome because the wood

fire had to be constantly watched and renewed.
Now the wood stove may be used for heating the
kitchen and for quick results, and all slow-cooking
processes completed in the fireless cooker.

COAL

In 1850 coal stoves for cooking began to be generally manufactured, and forty years later we find
the modern coal range with water-back connection
in almost every prosperous home except in the
country districts. As long as coal was reasonable
in price and domestic labor available for the average home, the coal range held its own. Its final
displacement is due to the same influences that
have brought automobiles into use instead of horses
— the demands of an age that must get the maximum quick results from the minimum effort.

The coal range is undoubtedly still a valuable resource under right conditions. But in the hands of
ignorant " help " or untrained housekeepers it is
ruinously wasteful of both fuel and time. Unless it
has expert management it does not do its work effectively; and it fills the kitchen with dust and dirt.
The most perfect types of coal range have now
overcome some of the disadvantages that cling to
the general class. Used in combination with a gas
stove the coal range can be run economically and
without waste of time, as the fire can be maintained at an even heat and the gas stove used for
emergency cooking, or when a very hot temperature is required for a short time. Baking can be

done when a fresh fire is made, or can be concentrated in one or two days a week when the fire is

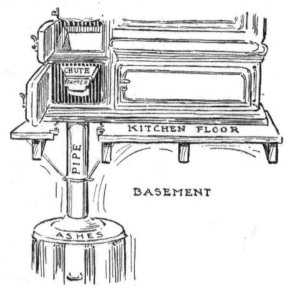

FIG. 11.—Shows lower portion of a coal range equipped with ash damper and chute to ash can in cellar.

run at a baking heat. At other times the small gas oven can be used to better advantage.

The best types of coal range are now equipped with oven thermometers, which are found accurate enough for practical purposes. Even housekeepers who have learned to cook by old-fashioned methods find these a great help.

A few ranges are so constructed that the ashes are emptied directly into a shaft beneath the grate leading to an ash can in the cellar. (See Fig. 11.) Both shaft and ash can are so enclosed as to confine all the dust. In this way the dirt of the coal range is taken out of the kitchen, and one of its worst disadvantages is overcome. Ranges not so constructed may be altered over by an ingenious mechanic. Directions for doing this are given in a recent bulletin of the Cornell Reading Course.

Coal stoves without water-back connections cost from $8.00 to $20.00. For ranges with water-backs the price is from $30.00 to $75.00. A range costing $35.00 will meet every need of the average home. For large families, boarding-houses and farm houses it is economy to get a good steel range of the best type and as free as possible from unnecessary ornamentation. Such a range will cost $75.00.

It is interesting to note that in some of the large railroad restaurants where the equipment is of the latest and most efficient kind, a coal range of the hotel type is included in the outfit. Gas stoves, gas broilers, etc., are used for all the processes needing quick results; but the coal range is relied on for the great volume of slow-cooking and baking operations and for broiling meats.

Consideration is given to the coal stove and its relation to the hot water heating problem, pages 71 to 73, in Chapter VI, on Hot Water Heating Systems.

GAS

It is not more than fifteen years since gas began to be used extensively as a kitchen fuel. Its advantages were first evident in those localities where natural gas was found, and could be piped direct to houses. Then it was discovered that gas could be manufactured from coal and used generally as a fuel throughout the United States. At first the process of manufacture was very expensive. Seventy years ago gas was sold in New York City for $7.00 per thousand feet. To-day the average price is $1.00 a thousand. In many places it is as low as eighty cents; and a St. Louis firm recently advertised it for fifty cents! Where the cost is one dollar a thousand or less it is more economical than coal for the kitchen, because its use can be more easily regulated from the point of view of economy.

Even after gas had been proved to be an economical and efficient fuel, and excellent stoves had been put on the market, it made its way but slowly in private homes, because of the conservatism and prejudice against an innovation. Then gas stoves began to be used in Western kitchens without the coal range. Finally vigorous campaigns of education were conducted by gas companies in the East, until the old prejudice was replaced by an active interest in the new fuel. The development of the fireless cook stove and steam cooker has also added greatly to the natural advantages of gas for cooking.

To sum up the various points in which gas has been helpful in solving the home-maker's problem of efficiency:

1. It is a clean fuel, being wholly free from dust and ashes, and requires the minimum care to keep the stove in good condition.
2. It can be used as needed, the expense stopping instantly when the burner is turned off.
3. It conserves the time of the worker, being always ready for quick results.
4. It is easy to handle and gives good results, even when used with only mediocre intelligence.
5. With study and intelligent use it gives uniform results, and develops a high degree of efficiency.

The choice of a gas stove is determined by the size of the family and the amount of income. A great number of very good stoves are on the market, and in such variety that every need can be met. For a home where only a minimum expense can be incurred $7.00 will buy a three-burner Junior gas stove with oven. (See Figs. 19 and 20.) A family able to afford a more lavish kitchen can spend $100 for the latest type of gas range with insulated oven. Most of the companies provide also for the needs of the renting class by offering gas ranges at a very moderate yearly rental.

ELECTRICITY

Electricity has very many of the advantages of gas, and in addition does not exhaust the oxygen in the air. It can also be installed in smaller space than the gas stove requires. Its chief drawbacks at present are the high price of the electric current and the costliness of electric equipment. The former problem is being solved in some communities. In certain parts of England electricity for cooking purposes has been offered at a rate of one cent per kilo-watt hour. This is unheard of in the United States, where ten cents is an average rate, and twelve or fifteen not at all unusual. In only a few favored localities is as low a rate as five cents offered.

The high price of electric appliances for cooking is partly due to the necessity for using only the best materials, such as nickel and copper in their manufacture; partly also to the fact that they must be well and skilfully made. Electric ranges at present cost from $60 to $125; and small appliances are proportionately expensive. The excellent quality of these utensils will, however, be a great advantage in the long run, once the problem of the rate of current has been solved. A very perfect electric fireless cooker has been lately put on the market. The first cost is high compared with the price of other fireless cookers. But it enables the housekeeper who employs no maid to do her cooking with the maximum economy of time and fuel. This cooker can be operated with great advantage wherever the rate does not exceed seven cents per kilo-watt hour.

KEROSENE

The cheapness of kerosene and the development of good types of blue-flame kerosene stoves have made this fuel a great resource in communities where it is not possible to obtain gas. When used in connection with a fireless cooker and a steamer,

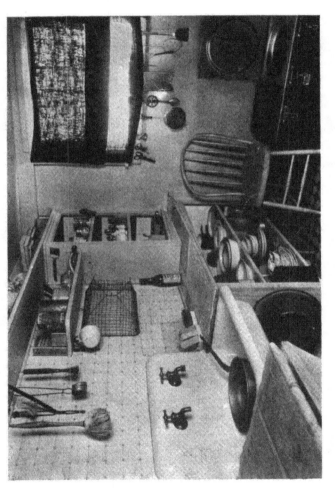

Convenient country kitchenette. Wilton, Conn. Laundry tub at left. Storage space for utensils well planned. Fireless-cooker at right. Blue flame kerosene range opposite sink

a good three-burner kerosene stove with a two-burner portable oven (Fig. 19) is sufficient to meet the needs of a family of five or six people.

There are two types of stove, those having wicks and those without; and a great many makes of each type. Some are good and some are not worth buying. Indeed there is no part of the kitchen equipment more important to choose with care than the kerosene stove and oven.

The best manufacturers carry a very complete repair stock, so that worn-out parts may be renewed. These stoves need intelligent care, and those with wicks must have the wicks frequently renewed. Otherwise they burn with a disagreeable odor. The inside of the enameled drum protecting the flame should be wiped out weekly and left thoroughly dry. The burner parts must be taken off and brushed with a stiff brush to prevent clogging. Especial care should be taken not to let liquids boil over and run down into the burners.

A highly perfected cooking device which may be run by kerosene is the Aladdin oven. In this the cooking is done inside an insulated oven, sixteen by fourteen by seventeen inches. The oven is heated by means of a large kerosene lamp or a Bunsen burner. This oven has not been used as extensively as it deserved on account of the cost, which is in the neighborhood of $25.00. This often seems to housekeepers prohibitive when so many kerosene utensils are offered for very much less.

It should be remembered, however, that first cost is only one of many considerations in deciding whether one article is really cheaper than another. Efficiency, operating cost, satisfactory service in the long run are factors infinitely more important. And this is particularly true of the more permanent utensils and equipment of the kitchen. When home-makers realize this they will be willing to economize on unessential things, and will gladly pay higher prices for honest tools which are really efficient for the work they are supposed to do.

Kerosene of the right specific gravity is a safe fuel when used with ordinary precautions. The law in the several states regulates the specific gravity; and the housekeeper herself must exercise the necessary precautions. The stove should never be filled when it is lighted; nor should it be left lighted when the housekeeper goes out. Food that needs long cooking may be finished in the fireless cooker and the kerosene flame turned out. It is also important to keep the kerosene in a safe place outside the house and beyond the reach of the children.

DENATURED ALCOHOL

Denatured alcohol may be used under the same conditions as kerosene, and in addition is a very desirable fuel for dining-room cooking and for light housekeeping. (See Chapter XI.)

Being cleaner than kerosene, and also free from unpleasant odors, it can be used in a tiny kitchenette as well as in an ordinary kitchen. Its efficiency is about equal to that of kerosene, when the best type of alcohol stove is compared to the best type

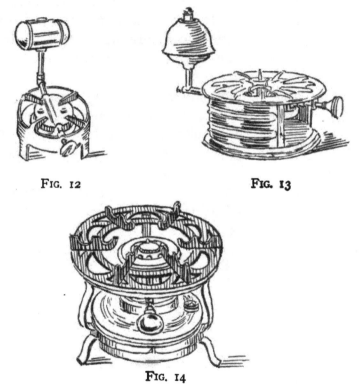

FIG. 12   FIG. 13

FIG. 14

FIGS. 12 and 14 are types of small alcohol stove adapted for dining-room use and light-housekeeping. FIG. 13 is especially suited for supplementary kitchen use.

of kerosene stove. There are many worthless stoves on the market, and great care must be used in selecting a type that has been thoroughly tested. The cost of denatured alcohol when bought by the barrel ranges from forty cents a gallon up to seventy-five cents in certain parts of the country. If it could be put on the market at a more reasonable figure as it is in Germany, it would prove a great resource in farming communities. At its present price it cannot compare with kerosene for cheapness, kerosene averaging ½c per hour, and alcohol 1½ cents.

The best alcohol stove for kitchen use is the wickless type. This comes in two-burner, portable form, and should be placed on a cabinet base. A separate single-burner stove ought to be purchased in addition. (See Figs. 12, 13 and 14.) A well insulated two-burner oven, a fireless cooker and a steamer are needed to make the equipment complete and efficient.

VIII

SELECTING THE FIXED EQUIPMENT

IN Chapters I and III we have shown how to so locate the fixed equipment of the kitchen that it will best conserve the energy and time of the worker. Now we come to an equally important consideration, the selection of the equipment itself. The four kitchen accessories which cost the most money and on which, more than any others, the comfort of the worker depends, are the sink, stove, work-table and refrigerator. Two of these, the sink and the stove, are usually supplied by the landlord in the rented house. But as they are often defective and need attention and replacing, it is highly important for the home-maker, whether she rents or owns her own home, to thoroughly understand the principles which make for efficiency in these two important adjuncts to the modern kitchen.

The sink ought to be of a material that is easily kept clean. It should have open plumbing, and should be set at a convenient height for the worker. The best height for a woman 5 feet 2 inches tall is to have the working surface of the sink set 27 inches from the floor. A sink which rests on legs is almost always too low; so it is best to get the type which is attached to the wall by concealed hangers. (See Fig. 15.) To properly strengthen the wall for this purpose have a board of the proper size and thickness nailed to the studs from which to suspend the hangers.

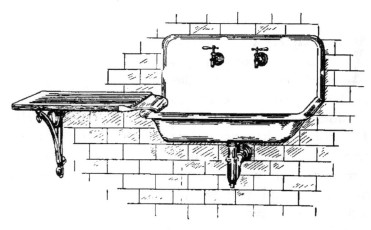

FIG. 15.— White enameled wall-type of sink, size 20 x 30, attached to wall by concealed hangers. Also comes with combination faucet and double drain-boards.

The cost of fitting and installing any kind of sink is about eight dollars, and may be more if the plumbing connection is complicated. This estimate is based on allowing $1.50 for the faucets, $3.50 for the trap and $3.00 for the connection. To this must be added the cost of the sink itself and the drain-boards.

Sinks now come in galvanized iron, wrought iron, soapstone, slate, white enameled-ware and crockery. The galvanized iron are the cheapest and least desirable of all, being very difficult to keep clean. Next come the iron sinks, which cost about $2.00. They were universally used a few years ago and are easily cleaned and sanitary; but are unattractive in appearance and require much more care than either the soap-stone, slate, enameled-ware or crockery. They are usually set in a frame of wood, covered with zinc. The zinc is carried up at the back to protect the wall. This is the work of a carpenter and costs from $2.00 to $4.00 extra.

For country houses where a large sink is desired a soap-stone or slate sink is the best. For farm houses the soap-stone would be preferable. A soap-stone sink with splasher back costs from $12.00 to $16.00. For the ordinary home and the average sized kitchen a sink of white enameled ware is the best choice. This sink, in a reliable grade, costs $8.00 for a size 20 by 30. A still better grade, wall type and with combination faucets, and splasher back, costs $22.00. The $8.00 sink will cost, installed, about $16.00, and the $22.00 sink about $30.00. To this must be added from $4.00 to $10.00 for drain-boards. Crockery sinks cost from $40.00 to $100.00, and so are possible only in wealthy homes.

It is important to protect the enameled-ware or crockery sink from scratches, by a wooden rack or rubber mat which may rest in the sink through the day. At night the rack may be removed and aired.

While the cost of an iron sink, when properly

encased in a frame and protected at back and on drain-boards with zinc, will not be far from the cost of the inexpensive grade of enameled-ware, they will stand harder service and would be better for the farm house than the enameled-ware. However the soap-stone meets that need so well that other types are hardly worth while considering. In some farm houses the sinks are made of copper and there are two set side by side. One is used for washing the dirty dishes and the other for scalding or rinsing dishes. This is an excellent plan where there are many dishes to be washed and proves a great advantage also in boarding-houses. The second sink has many uses besides that of scalding the dishes. It is invaluable for cleaning and preparing vegetables. Many things like spinach, which require abundant rinsing, could be handled with great facility with such an arrangement. Such sinks are found in the kitchenettes of dining-cars on the Pullman system and are made of German silver. An immense amount of dish-washing is done by one person in a very short time. In these kitchenettes there is no room for storing dirty dishes. Everything must be washed up immediately and put away.

It is a great convenience in a kitchen to have ample drain-boards, preferably at both left hand and right. But if only one is possible it should be placed on the left hand side. Sometimes there is room for a small one on the right and a long one on the left. With this arrangement the dishes can be piled up on the right hand end ready to wash. Where there is not room for even a small drain-board on the right side, a table on castors or a wheel cart may be used instead. It is best to avoid handling anything more than once, so the wheel cart should hold its load until all the dishes have been transferred to the dish-pan.

Wooden drain-boards are usually made of ash, and oiled. They are not very attractive in appearance; so many housekeepers prefer the enameled-ware ones to match the sink.

Some housekeepers have the ash drain-boards painted white and enameled. This is possible in kitchens where the work is done deftly but would not be practical for the average kitchen where the boards get hard wear. Zinc-covered drain-boards are the most satisfactory where durability is an essential. A cheaper grade of wood may be selected where they are to be covered with zinc.

The sink should have open plumbing so that it is always possible to get at the pipes and so that the light and air can keep everything clean. The connection with the waste pipe is made by means of a trap (a bend in the pipe devised to retain enough water to act as a seal and prevent the passage of foul air back into the room).

Figures 16 and 17 show two types of trap in common use. Figure 18 shows a trap not properly constructed. If the water does not stand at least

one inch in the bend it is likely to evaporate and
fall below the bend and thus break the seal.

Plumbers tell us that very few housekeepers
realize the importance of flushing the pipes with

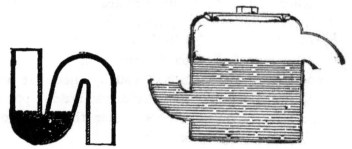

Figs. 16 and 17 are known as S-trap and bottle-trap. The
water standing above bend is called the water seal.

Fig. 18 represents a defective S-trap. The water does not
rise above the bend and permits foul gases to get out into
the room.

Note.— Reprinted by courtesy of Whitcomb & Barrows
from "House Sanitation," by Marion Talbot.

plenty of hot water every day. If this were done,
and if proper precautions were taken to prevent an
excessive amount of grease from getting into the
dish water, there would be very few cases of
stopped-up sinks and no unpleasant odors.

For various reasons fully explained in Chapters VI and VII, new kitchens are being fitted up with gas stoves and separate water-heating systems instead of the customary coal range with water-back connection. This is because the gas stove is free from dust and ashes and requires less skill to handle, and because its heat is available the instant it is needed. In country kitchens where gas is not available kerosene or alcohol stoves are practical for small families, used in connection with a good fireless cook-stove and steamer. For large families where it is desirable to retain the coal range it will be found an economy of time and fuel to purchase a gas or kerosene stove for supplementary use in cooking. It is often necessary to heat something up quickly when the coal range is banked for the afternoon; instead of starting up the range or going without what one wants, the small stove can be lighted and used instead. It is not to be recommended to replace the coal stove with gas, unless both the heating and hot-water problems are properly solved. In houses where the heating system is adequate it is not a vital matter to have the kitchen heated, but in a large majority of cases, the houses are poorly built and equipped with inadequate furnaces and would be very uncomfortable without the extra heat from the coal stove. It should also be remembered that provision must be made for heating the house in the late spring and early fall when furnace heat is only needed part of the day. These provisions having been made, the next question to decide is what make of gas stove to select.

Gas stoves of such excellent make are on the market, and in such great variety, that it is possible to find something especially suitable for each kitchen and at a price that any one can afford. To give some idea of the range of choice we have divided the different types into groups, giving with each group the approximate price and the outfit that should be purchased in order to use the gas most economically. The gas kitchen is never complete without the fireless cooker, and while this is not included in each group it is understood to be a necessary part of the outfit.

Gas stoves have been long enough on the market to furnish the home-maker with one· of the surest of all tests for reliability, " the test of time." Unless you can secure reliable information about new makes it will be best to select a stove made by a well known and reliable firm. And they manufacture among them almost every known type of stove, fitted to every need and condition. Certain special features may be found in one make and not in another, so it is a good plan to look the field over before you make your choice. Your local dealer can get any type that you prefer, but he will generally try to get you to buy something that he has in stock, irrespective of whether or not it is for your best interest.

It is not wise as a rule to send too far away for

your stove, because long distance negotiations are inconvenient in case of defects or necessary repairs.

In general the features of a gas stove to be especially noted are the following:

1. Good burners that can be adjusted to varying pressure of gas permit economical use.
2. Good construction. Best stoves are made of steel and have ovens insulated with two layers of asbestos with dead air space between.
3. Simplicity of design. No elaborate ornamentation which requires time and labor for polishing.
4. Good-sized oven. An 18-inch oven is very superior to a 16-inch, promoting economy in baking.
5. Elevated oven and broiler, to prevent awkward and trying bending over.
6. Provision for carrying off fumes of gas, either by connection with flue or by means of small register and hood for ventilation.
7. Facilities for warming dishes. In some types of range this need is provided for. In smaller stoves special supplementary arrangements may be made. See pages 68 and 69, Chapter V.
8. Proper location to insure good light.
9. Proper height.
10. Proper fire protection for wall back of stove.
11. Fire protection under stove.

The following conveniences add to the attractiveness and price of gas stoves, but do not increase their efficiency:

1. Glass doors, convenient for watching the progress of baking, but easily broken by draughts of cold air on over-heated glass.
2. White enameled lining to oven, drip-pan and broiler.
3. Additional oven. Ranges having a small and a large oven, convenient and desirable in small families doing much entertaining and for large families.
4. Special reflector arrangement which acts as an index if oven light goes out. (Does not add to expense, only found in one make.)
5. Special arrangement of burners, differing in different makes.

VARIOUS TYPES OF GAS STOVE AND THE COST

I. Three-burner Junior gas stove with portable oven (see Figs. 19 and 20), costing about $7.00. This gives very efficient service, and, used in connection with the fireless cooker and steamer, will meet the needs of a large family. It should be placed on a cabinet base, covered with zinc, and having a place for the portable oven and steamer conveniently at hand.

II. A four-burner oven range, either plain type with oven below burners (illustrated in plate) or with elevated oven. (See Fig. 21.) Costs from $18.00 to $25.00.

III. Four-burner cabinet range with one oven and broiler. (See plate.) Provides a place for

FIG. 19.— Double portable oven to be used with Junior gas stove, alcohol or kerosene stoves.

warming dishes on top shelf above oven. $25.00 to $30.00.

IV. Combination gas and coal stove. Recommended for houses where coal stove must be used to heat water supply and heat kitchen. $58.00.

FIG. 20.— Junior gas stove, the simplest and least expensive type of gas stove.

V. Combination gas and fireless cook-stove. Two kinds:

1. Consists of wooden cabinet containing compartments for fireless cooker and its utensils

with a four-burner gas stove above. This kind of combination gas and fireless cooker has a gas stove just like any other gas stove. The elevated

FIG. 21.— A four-burner standard oven range with elevated oven and broiler. A very desirable type.

baking oven with warming oven above and broiling oven below is located at the right-hand side and the four top burners are on the left-hand side. The cabinet on which the stove rests is made of weathered oak instead of iron or steel, and contains a compartment for storing the utensils to the fireless cooker and two open compartments in which the fireless cookers remain when not in use. This combination is very useful as a space-saver, giving one the advantage of both a large gas stove and a large fireless cooker.

2. A gas stove having a special insulated oven,

and equipped with hoods which can be lowered over the open burners on the top of the stove and act as heat-retaining compartments, is also on the market.   It is very much liked and gives unusually good results in baking because of the perfect insulation of the oven.   It is expensive and therefore beyond the means of the average family, but where it can be afforded it will be economical in operating expenses and will be a great satisfaction to housekeepers who wish to secure accurate results in baking.   It costs from $35.00 to $175.00.   One suited to the average family of five costs $65.00.

VI. The Aladdin Oven is an invention that has been on the market for twenty years and can be operated either by gas or kerosene.   It has been thoroughly tested by many cooking schools.   It is a heat-retaining cooking box with well insulated walls so that a temperature of 400 degrees may be maintained in the oven.   Height including stand is 4 ft., width 21 ins., depth 16½.   Inside dimensions of oven 16 by 17 by 14.   There are three shelves in the oven and a drop door.   The cost of cooking in this oven is very low and the results very perfect. One would need a three-burner gas stove to complete the outfit if the Aladdin oven is purchased. Cost, $25.00.

KEROSENE AND ALCOHOL STOVES

The desirability of kerosene and alcohol as fuels has been discussed in Chapter VII.   While a number of cheap stoves of each kind are on the market they cannot be recommended as being economical to purchase where length of service is required. They may do for a season's use or two, but for a permanent investment we recommend only stoves of the best make.

Blue-flame kerosene stoves come in two, three and four-burner type, and in either the portable form or on cabinet bases. The cost of a reliable make with oven will be around $15.00.

The alcohol stove is made at present only in one and two-burner portable types. It is desirable to have a special cabinet made with zinc-covered top on which the stove may rest. Shelves underneath hold the portable oven, steamers, etc., used with the stove. For general use one needs at least three burners. This may be secured by purchasing a two-burner type for kitchen use exclusively and a one-burner type in either kitchen or dining-room type. (See page 97, Figs. 12, 13 and 14.) The former costs $9.00, and the latter may be secured from $1.50 to $4.50.

COAL RANGES

Coal stoves of very simple design may be purchased for as low as $9, but a modern range, suited to the average needs of a family of five, cannot be secured for less than $20. From $20 to $45 one can find a great number of good makes, varying more in grade of material and excellence of construction and design than in outward appearance.

The price quoted on a range usually includes setting in position and in most cases the cost of the stove-pipe. Where this is not included in the price it will cost about $1.00 for stovepipe and two or three dollars for setting. If the range is to be equipped with a hot-water back one must allow five dollars extra, and from five to eight dollars to connect the range to the hot-water boiler. Five dollars is the average charge where the connection does not require extra piping or extra work. This price should include brass piping, but it is necessary to specify that this is desired, as in some localities iron piping is more commonly used.

Where unusually large ranges are needed, as for farms or boarding-houses, it often pays to get the best make of French steel range, which costs $75.00. It is not wise to make cost the first consideration, as it often pays to get a more expensive make that will insure economy of operation and last longer.

With a coal range one needs the following equipment:

	Cheap grade	Best grade
Poker	$ .10	$ .25
Rake for cleaning soot	.10	.25
Whisk broom	.25	.25
Blacking brush and dauber ...	.25	.75
Stove lifter	.10	.25
Shovel	.10	.25
Coal scuttle	.35	.60
Ash can	.50	3.00
Broiler	.25	.25
Ash sifter	.65	5.00
	$2.65	$10.85

An ash sifter, fitting over a barrel, or galvanized can, will pay for itself in a short time. It pays in this case where it is possible to buy the five-dollar kind, as it is so well made that it will last many years. It is much easier to operate than the little one, making the ash sifting a less dusty operation. It is needed for the furnace as well as for the range and laundry heater.

Gas stove outfit, needed to use gas with economy:

```
Small toaster ........................$ .25
3-compartment steamer ................. 2.00
Gas lighter ........................... .25
                                      _____
                                      $2.50
```

Kerosene stove outfit:

```
1 gallon and one 5-gallon can ..........$1.20
Toaster ............................... .25
Steamer ............................... 2.00
                                      _____
                                      $3.45
```

Alcohol outfit:

```
Small and large can ...................$1.25
Pourer ................................ .15
Toaster ............................... .25
Steamer ............................... 2.00
                                      _____
                                      $3.65
```

Summary:

```
Cheapest reliable coal-stove and outfit....$22.65
Cheapest reliable gas stove and outfit....  9.50
Cheapest reliable alcohol stove and outfit.. 17.65
Cheapest reliable kerosene stove and outfit. 16.95
```

NOTE.— A special top for gas stoves is on the market called a " heat controller," which distributes the heat of one burner so that the whole top is heated and available for cooking. Two sections are needed for a four-burner stove.

THE WORK-TABLE AND ITS ACCESSORIES

The advantages of having the work-table so arranged that the wall space back of it may be available for shelves was spoken of in the chapter on "Built-in Conveniences" (pages 48 to 51). The convenience and desirability of this arrangement cannot be over-emphasized. In fact, the type of table selected is of far less importance than the proper placing of it so that the worker has her supplies conveniently at hand and a good light to work by.

The cheapest kitchen table is one measuring 36 inches and selling for about $2.50. Such a table has a single drawer for cutlery. The top may be covered with a good grade of table oil-cloth, but it is advisable to have it covered with zinc. This adds about $1.75 to the cost, but it will be found worth the difference in price because the various labor-saving utensils may be clamped to the edge without disfiguring the table.

Much more convenient than the ordinary kitchen table is the Pastry Table of the same size, shown in the illustration facing page 44. Pastry tables have two drawers for cutlery, two pastry boards to pull out, and two bins for different kinds of flour underneath. The flour bins are zinc-lined. These tables cost about $8.00, and may be covered with either zinc or white enamel, as preferred. This adds from $1.75 to $2.75 to the cost. The zinc is recommended for ordinary conditions, as this table gets hard wear.

A pastry table like this, with two narrow shelves above it, can be used in almost any kitchen. It is a good investment for the home-maker who must live in rented houses, because both the table and shelves can be easily carried about and adapted to different conditions.

KITCHEN CABINETS

These are especially desirable for families who do not own their own homes. They should, in fact, be considered a necessity in families who are unable to have permanent home centers. A well designed kitchen cabinet will make almost any kitchen convenient. A number of excellent designs are on the market, and equipped with every kind of convenience imaginable. As there is such great variety to choose from, and as some of the appointments especially appeal to certain housekeepers and do not appeal to others, it is important to get the particular type you will like to use for a lifetime, and cost is a secondary consideration. Very expensive types have the inside of the cabinet painted with white enamel and a white porcelain enamel pastry board or "bake board," as it is sometimes called. These cost in the neighborhood of $50.00. A very desirable type can be bought for $27.50.

A well made kitchen cabinet must be made of good wood, well-seasoned. The finish also adds · to its cost, but the most important consideration is the wood. Poorly seasoned wood warps and swells and is a constant annoyance in opening and closing drawers. Another point to remember in selecting a cabinet is the outfit of utensils that go with the different types. For à housekeeper fitting out with everything new a cabinet containing a complete list of containers will save her at least $10.00 in the utensils she will have to purchase. If one already has this outfit a type of cabinet may be selected that does not include them, or one can buy the base alone and depend on having narrow shelves fastened to the wall above it to hold the supplies.

A home-made kitchen cabinet can be contrived with moderate expense, in families where the husband or brother is handy with tools, and where outside labor need not be called in. If both lumber and labor must be purchased, the cost will equal that of the ready-made cabinet. With a home-made cabinet the wall space can be used to the best possible advantage. The cost of building a cabinet of this kind will be approximately as follows:

```
Lumber  ................................$ 7.75
Labor  ..................................  8.00
Zinc for work-shelf ....................  1.75
                                        _____
                                         $17.50
```

Equipment needed to make this cabinet as complete as the manufactured ones on the market is enumerated in the following list:

```
1 25-lb. patent flour bin and sifter ..............$ 3.50
1 5-lb. container for pastry flour ................  .25
2 2-qt. glass jars for rye and entire wheat flour..  .20
```

```
1 2-lb. container oat-meal .....................  .15
1 8-lb. sugar container .......................  .50
½ doz. chemists' bottles with wide mouths and glass
      stoppers ................................. 1.25
6 pt. jars, various supplies....................  .45
9 qt. jars .....................................  .50
1 roll-top bread box ........................... 1.75
1 bread knife .................................  .50
1 cake box ....................................  .75
2 stone crocks for crackers ...................  .90
                                               --------
                                                $10.70
```

The total cost of such an open-shelf cabinet and its equipment will be around $28.00 if all the lumber and labor must be paid for. It may exceed this cost if extra drawers and compartments are made. When the lumber is on hand and the work can be done by some member of the family, or where the equipment is already part of the present kitchen outfit, it may save considerable expense to use what one has instead of buying a ready-made one. In many cases the available space in a kitchen can be utilized to far better advantage by building a cabinet than by using a ready-made one. It thus becomes a question of expediency.

THE REFRIGERATOR

"There are two questions which almost every woman asks when she buys a refrigerator," said a representative of one of the best refrigerator companies the other day, "and neither of these has anything to do with the problem of refrigeration. One question relates to the outside finish, and the other to the appearance of the inside." The first essential in a good refrigerator, the most important consideration, is its construction, insuring perfect insulation and circulation of air-currents. The outside casing is only important as regards durable, seasoned wood or metal, with tight fitting joints.

As the whole value of the refrigerator lies in its maintaining a low and uniform temperature, this matter of insulation is of the first importance. To thoroughly protect the inside of the refrigerator from atmospheric conditions it is necessary that the outer wooden or metal case be lined with several layers of non-conducting material with a dead air space between. The best refrigerators have from eight to twelve such layers. Refrigerators so constructed can maintain a temperature of 40 to 42 degrees, whereas inferior makes maintain only 50 degrees and very poor ones 60 degrees.

The second essential is good circulation of air currents. Low temperature in a refrigerator is a result of the melting of ice. The air in the ice compartment becomes chilled and passes downward to the compartment below, its place being taken by warm air from the adjoining food compartment. This process takes place in any refrigerator, but it can be greatly improved by a type of construction designed to accelerate and direct the air currents. Certain types produce such perfect circulation that the air is not only chilled but freed from moisture in passing from one compartment to another. A dry, cold air is the ideal condition for preserving food. Fig. 22 shows the natural passage of air currents in a refrigerator. This natural action is

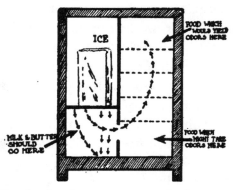

FIG. 22.— Sketch showing movement of air currents in a refrigerator. The compartment directly below ice chamber is the coolest; the air here has been purified by passing over the ice.

(Reprinted by courtesy of the *Housefurnishing Review*.)

facilitated in some refrigerators by the use of innumerable syphons in the wall between the ice compartment and adjoining food compartment.

Third essential. To insure the maximum efficiency, the refrigerator must be kept well filled with ice. Therefore a refrigerator with large ice capacity results in a heavy ice-bill, whether it is used for a large or a small family. This ice consumption cannot wisely be checked by wrapping the ice in paper or heavy cloth, as this defeats the fundamental principle of refrigeration. The only way to run the refrigerator economically is to keep it full of ice. If the air in the ice chamber is kept at the lowest possible temperature, it will maintain its level of 40° in the other compartments and there will be no warm air to melt the ice. If, however, the ice supply gets greatly reduced, the temperature in the food

FIG. 23.— This type of refrigerator permits the best circulation of air and affords the best storage facilities. Dimensions: width 33 inches, depth 19¼ inches, height 48½ inches; ice capacity 75 pounds.

compartments will rise and the melting will be more rapid than if a low temperature throughout had been maintained.

The best policy therefore is to select a refrigerator of such a size that you can afford to keep it full of ice.

For the average family who must consider carefully the cost of ice and secure the maximum efficiency for the least daily outlay, a refrigerator of

65 lbs. ice capacity will give good results.   In order
to insure perfect circulation of air, choose the type
having the ice chamber on one side (see Fig. 23),
one food chamber below it, and two food chambers

FIG. 24.— Type of refrigerator needed in kitchenettes and
apartment houses.

on the other side.   In small kitchens and apartments it is often necessary, for economy of space,
to get the type that has the ice chamber above and
one food compartment below.   (See Fig. 24.)   A
refrigerator of this type, about twenty-five inches
wide and a little over four feet high, of a reliable
make and zinc lined, costs about $17.00.   The
same type with porcelain-enamel lining, will be at
least ten dollars more.   The double type, which
gives the best circulation and larger storage facilities, in the porcelain enamel lining will cost about

$56.00. Five dollars additional must be allowed if you want to have the rear or end outside icing door. This is a great convenience, as it makes it unnecessary for the ice-man to come into the kitchen to deliver the ice. It also enables one to use the refrigerator six months of the year without ice, the cold air from the outside producing the refrigeration.

The improper location of the refrigerator causes more wasted effort than any other defect of the kitchen arrangement. Tradition says the refrigerator must not be in the kitchen, but in some cooler place. In these days, however, tradition is giving way to the necessity of conserving human energy. Moreover, several new factors are affecting the situation, the most important of which is the great improvement in the construction of refrigerators with perfect insulation. The temperature within is not affected by outside conditions, unless through carelessness the refrigerator door is left open. This is well illustrated in the tiny kitchenettes of the Pullman system, where the refrigerators are placed within a few feet of the kitchen range.

The best grades of refrigerators are made with rear or end doors to allow icing from the outside. Not only does this save the kitchen from the tracking in of dirt by the ice-man but it makes the refrigerator available six months of the year without ice. Where the circulation system is good, the air keeps as sweet and fresh without ice in cold weather as when ice is used. It is necessary to protect the opening outside with a fine screen to keep out the dust.

Another very desirable convenience is an arrangement for cooling the drinking water. A coil of block tin pipe is placed in the bottom of the ice chamber, having one end connected with the city water supply and terminating at the other end in a faucet. The water is thus kept ice-cold without the disadvantage of having the ice melted in it. The cost of this installation is from $14.00 to $25.00, depending on the size of the refrigerator.

The drain pipe of the refrigerator should be connected with a separate pipe, emptying into a dry well in the grounds. It should never be connected with the sewer pipe. Where it is not possible to make a separate pipe connection, an ingenious little device can be made under the refrigerator to insure the drip pan always remaining in the right location under the outlet. Mark on the floor the right location of the pan and then tack two strips to the floor on either side of the pan. When the pan is pushed in and out it will always be under the outlet and the floor will never get wet from the overflow.

Every manufacturer or salesman of high-grade refrigerators should be able to guarantee the following requirements:

1. That a low and uniform temperature can be maintained, preferably 40 to 42 degrees F.

2. Perfect circulation, producing a pure atmosphere, freedom from odors and freedom from moisture.

3. Ease in keeping every part in absolutely sanitary condition, insured by seamless porcelain-enamel lining or nickel.

4. Perfect drainage.

5. Economy in the consumption of ice.

To run the refrigerator economically the following points should be borne in mind:

1. Food should be cooled before putting on ice. A screened shelf or closet above refrigerator, makes a good temporary place for hot foods, while cooling.

2. Keep the ice chamber full of ice.

3. Every time the box is filled, take out the piece of ice remaining, wipe out compartment with a clean cloth wet in hot soapy water. Wipe off box. Have the new supply in one block of ice as large as the box will carry.

4. The ice chamber should not be used for food.

5. Examine contents of refrigerator daily and dispose of anything not likely to be used in a day or two.

6. Be careful to wipe up at once anything that is spilled in food compartment.

7. Butter, milk and eggs, which readily absorb odors, should be placed in the compartment directly below ice chamber. This compartment, besides receiving air purified from

passage over the ice, is also the coolest compartment. Cantaloupes, onions or other supplies giving off odors can be placed in the other compartments without contaminating the milk. This is true of refrigerators having proper circulation and of the double type. In cheap refrigerators strong food should not be kept at all.

IX

LISTS OF NECESSARY EQUIPMENT

ANY one who has seen the beautiful kitchen in Washington's home at Mount Vernon must have been impressed by the great change that has come to the home in the last hundred years in the matter of cooking utensils. The heavy polished copper vessels suggested a great hotel rather than a home; yet they were the kind and shape that were then in common use. In simpler homes they were made of iron instead of copper, because of the saving in expense. To-day we have the light, attractive aluminum and agate ware, and block tin where aluminum cannot be afforded. The size of utensils is greatly reduced, the variety and number greatly multiplied.

In Colonial days the outfit was suited to large families and many servants. Fireplace cooking was the rule until the first very primitive coal stove was invented. Now we have far more complex and perfect stoves, of many types and varieties, finally reaching the most complex of all, the electrical apparatus. Hired service in the majority of homes is reduced to one person, and time has become a vital consideration. Under these new

conditions rapid and skilful work and labor-saving
equipment are the chief necessities.   So inventions
are being constantly brought out to save loss of
time, energy and fuel.   The idea of conservation
was first brought into prominence by the manufacture of the fireless cooker.   This is an adaptation
of the old Norwegian hay box.   The idea of conservation of time, of energy and fuel, of all costly
commodities, is now the keynote of perfect kitchen
equipment.

There are two chief things to remember in deciding upon our equipment.   The first is to keep
the equipment as simple as possible and not to get
anything that we do not really need.   The second
seems the opposite of this.   Namely, to make our
equipment save our time and have it ample enough
so that no time is wasted through lack of efficient
tools.   Families differ very much in the scale and
manner of living.   Therefore any list that will
meet the average need inevitably includes many
things that are necessary to some housekeepers and
superfluous to others.   The lists given therefore
are intended to be suggestive, and not to give hard
and fast rules.   They are so grouped that it will
be easy to omit the equipment that is not needed
in a given case.   If, for instance, bread is bought
at the bakery, all the bread-making outfit may be
omitted.   The same if pie-making, cake-making
or any sort of fancy cooking is cut off the list.   So
many of these things are now being made very sat-

isfactorily outside the home, that it is often better policy to buy than to make them.

The prices given for equipment also cannot be completely accurate, as they vary somewhat in different parts of the country and there are many grades and makes of certain articles. We have therefore included in one list an outfit which may

FIG. 25.—Standard measuring cup used in all recipes.

FIG. 26.—Accurate household scales should be found in every kitchen.

be purchased for the minimum price, in the other the outfit which we recommend where economy does not have to be considered. We advise every housekeeper to have the full list of labor-saving equipment of a good grade bought of a reliable firm. The housekeeper of small income needs this even more than the one with ample means. Where the amount of money that can be spent on equipment is limited, we advise buying most of the smaller things at the 5 and 10. cent stores, reserving enough money to buy the best grade of expensive articles. A well insulated fireless cooker with aluminum utensils ought to last a life time, a wheel-cart will pay for itself in a short time in the energy it saves. In some homes a good mayonnaise mixer may be more important than anything else on the list, and so it goes. Whenever any household task seems a burden, look about and see if there is not some article on the market that will reduce the labor or make the work more perfect. Even poorly cut bread may be a cause of daily friction. How much easier to purchase a

FIG. 27.— Represents one type of oven thermometer. Costs from $1.50 to $6.00 depending on range and accuracy.

bread slicer for 75 cents than to daily chide a careless maid.

Remember that labor-saving equipment is disposition-saving as well, and try to so equip your kitchen that accurate, skilful work can be done with the minimum strain and weariness. Too much cannot be said in favor of equipment promoting accuracy in measurement. Insist upon careful measurements in all recipes. (The standard measuring cup for all recipes is illustrated in Fig. 25.) Have weighing scales (see Fig. 26) and cultivate the habit of using them. Weigh the flour used in bread-making, the ingredients of cakes and puddings. Learn to use an oven thermometer (see Fig. 27), keeping careful record on the receipt cards of cooking temperatures required for different foods.

SIMPLEST AND LEAST EXPENSIVE EQUIPMENT
FOR A FAMILY OF FIVE

Articles to group near stove:

Tea-kettle	$ .50
Salt box	.10
Pepper shaker	.05
Flour dredger	.05
Pot covers, three	.30
Large cast iron frying pan	.60
Small wrought iron frying pan	.25
Match box	.10
Box for burnt matches	.05
Stove cloths	.10
Dripping pans, two	.40
Griddle	.60
	$3.10

Sink outfit:

Scrubbing pail	$ .20
Scrubbing brush	.15
Sink shovel	.10
Sink strainer	.10
Sink brush	.05
Soap dish	.10
Dish mop	.10
Soap shaker	.18
Glass holder	.05
Plate scraper	.10
Dish pan	.50
Agate hand basin	.20
Wire dish mop	.10
Dish drainer	.30
Bottle cleaning brush	.25
Funnel	.05
	$2.53

Articles to group near sink:

Stew pans, 1 1-qt., 1 2-qt., 1 3-qt., 1 4-qt.	$1.00
Large 8-qt. agate preserving kettle	1.35

Pitchers, 1 2-qt., 1 1½-qt., 1 1-qt., 3 small ones.... 1.25
Tea-pot .... .15
Tea canister .... .10
Coffee pot, or stew-pan specially reserved for coffee
    making .... .25
Coffee canister .... .10
2 strainers .... .40
Double boiler .... .75
Colander .... .25
2 meas. cups .... .10

                                                $5.70

Work table, 36-inch with one drawer.............$2.50
Stool or chair .... .50
Pastry board .... .30

                                             $3.30

✓   Cooking dishes to group near work table:

2 meas. cups (duplicate set) ....$ .20
2 small white bowls .... .22
2 larger bowls .... .40
Wooden spoons (2) .... .10
Perforated cake spoon .... .10
Tin sugar box .... .10
Tin flour box .... .10
Wire egg whip .... .10
Crank egg beater .... .25
Grater .... .10
Potato masher .... .10
Biscuit cutters, 2 sizes .... .10
Pie tins (2) .... .12
Layer cake tins (3) .... .30
Gem pans, 2 of 12 holes each .... .20
Bread pans (3) .... .60
Lemon squeezer .... .05
Rolling pin .... .25
Chopping bowl and knife .... .45

                                             $3.84

Knife box outfit to go in cutlery drawer of table:

Knife box	$ .10
Can opener	.10
Cork screw	.10
3 kitchen forks	.30
3 kitchen knives	.30
1 doz. aluminum teaspoons	.60
6 table-spoons	.60
Cake turner	.05
Apple-corer	.05
Vegetable knife	.15
Knife sharpener	.25

$2.60

Dishes to put food away in:

3 small agate dishes	$ .30
4 larger agate dishes ranging from 1 qt. capacity to 3 qts	.60
2 kitchen platters	.40
½ doz. kitchen plates	.50
Empty lard pails for grease, etc.	

$1.80

Containers for cooked food and supplies:

Bread box with knife and board	$ .80
Cake box	.25
Cracker box	.10
Butter jar	.10
1 doz. pint jars	.75
1 doz. quart jars..............................	.80

$2.80

Miscellaneous:

Clock	$1.00
Scissors	.25
Ice pick	.10
Garbage can	.50
Coffee mill	.35
Scales, 24 lbs.	1.25

$3.45

Cleaning outfit:

Floor mop ....$ .35
Broom .... .50
Whisk broom .... .25
Dust pan .... .10
Large scrubbing brush .... .25
Small scrubbing brush .... .20
2 broom covers made of canton flannel .... .20
2 cheese cloth dusters .... .10
Cleaning cloths made from old linen or 3 yds muslin .30
Floor cloths (2), use old shirts or buy 2 yds. outing
    flannel .... .12
Crash oven-cloths or holders .... .10
                                              _____
                                              $2.47

Kitchen linen outfit:

Dish towels, 12 at 10 cents each, made of cotton tow-
    eling at 10 cents a yd., or buy 1 doz. empty 100
    lb. flour sacks at 30 cents $1.20
½ doz. linen towels 1.20
4 dish cloths, made of loose unbleached muslin...... .20
4 roller towels, 2 yds. long, cheapest grade ...... .80
    Better grade advisable cost $1.60.
Heavy cloth bag for paper .... .15
                                              _____
                                              $3.55

Chest refrigerator to hold about 70 lbs. ice $13.00
Fireless cooker, 1 8-qt. and one 4-qt. well, terne-
    plate lining vent valve 14.25
Wheel cart 5.50
                                              _____
                                              $32.75

The following conveniences may be added to a
kitchen outfit without expense.

Useful molds for steaming brown-bread and puddings.

3 one-lb. empty baking powder tins, and 1 or 2
pound coffee cans.

3 and 5-lb. lard pails make splendid containers for
dried bread crumbs, grease, etc.

Tin boxes with hinged covers are useful for
cleaning preparations, and lunch boxes.

Good sized empty cracker boxes may be purchased for ten cents apiece, and make excellent
containers for cake and crackers.

Newspapers, brown paper, paper bags, wrapping
paper twine, and oiled paper have many uses in the
kitchen and should all be saved.

Salt and flour bags, ripped and washed, make
good dish cloths, and lettuce bags.   Narrow strips
of white muslin stitched together end for end, make
convenient bands to wrap around the edge of berry
pies to prevent juice from overflowing.

· Glass bacon jars may have covers preserved by
inserting edge of knife under cover to let air in.
The cover can then be removed easily.   These jars
are useful to hold mayonnaise, white of egg, sour
cream, etc.   They also make excellent jelly and
conserve glasses.

The total cost of least expensive outfit where '
stove, sink and hot-water heating systems are furnished by the landlord is therefore seen to be
$35.14 for necessities (groups 1 to 11) and $32.75
for articles like the ice-chest, fireless cooker, etc.,
which some housekeepers do not consider necessities, a total of $67.89.

Least. Expensive Equipment where stove, sink and hot-water heating apparatus must be included in cost.

Least expensive gas stove ....$ 7.00
Hot water heating system — small laundry heater
 in basement to heat water supply and furnish
 heat to kitchen, see method described on pages
 74–75 .... 31.50
Sink, moderate-priced white enamel, installed.... 16.00
Equipment, Groups 1 to 11 inclusive 35.14
Refrigerator, fireless cooker, etc., Group 12...... 32.75
               ———
              $122.39

We recommend buying this least expensive type of gas stove where economy must be considered, and for the same reason recommend the laundry-stove equipment, although the first cost of the latter is more than the cheapest form of gas heater. This is because the laundry stove may be utilized to heat the kitchen, because it enables one to do supplementary cooking in the cellar and because it keeps not only the cellar dry in summer, but indirectly keeps the whole house free from dampness. It may be operated at a cost of from 75 cents to $1.50 a month. This equipment is right in all its essentials, and includes two of the most important labor-savers. It may be added to as time goes on. The inexpensive gas stove may be replaced by a better one and the one replaced may be then used for a warming closet for dishes.

Where a kerosene or alcohol stove is used instead of gas, the equipment recommended would

be the same. Simply add the difference between
the cost of stove in each case. It will be approximately $7.00 more than the gas stove.

Where a coal range is to be used instead the
equipment will differ in two other essentials, as may
be seen from the following estimate:

Inexpensive coal range and outfit ....$ 22.65
Water back, 30 gallon galvanized iron boiler and
    installation 20.00
Sink, moderate-priced white enamel, installed 16.00
Equipment, Groups 1 to 11 inclusive 35.14
Refrigerator chest, etc 32.75

$126.54

SUMMARY

It will be seen from figures given that a kitchen
already equipped with a stove, sink and hot-water
heating system may be fitted out with necessities
for $35.14, and with a moderate-priced refrigera-
tor, fireless cooker and wheel cart, for $32.75 addi-
tional, a total of $67.89.

It will further be seen that it will cost from $55.00
to $65.00 (see pages 86-87) more than this to add a
stove, sink and hot-water heating system. Housekeepers who have not studied the question of kitchen
equipment in all its bearings may think that even
this amount is excessive. It is true thousands of
women get along with much less equipment than
this, but we are introducing a new requirement in
our standard when we insist on the efficiency of
the worker. To enable women to meet this new
requirement we must have better sink arrange-

ments and ample hot water for kitchen use as well as good equipment. With the equipment as given here the kitchen is fitted out to meet the average needs of a family of five, and with an additional laundry equipment, costing $15.00, to do the laundry work also.

LIBERAL EQUIPMENT FOR FAMILY OF FIVE

We shall now consider the cost of equipping a kitchen where the home-maker is not limited in expenditure, and where she may choose the equipment that is attractive in appearance as well as serviceable in the long run. This list includes many articles that save labor and time, and which will therefore prove an economy in operating expense. The equipment is the one in use at the Housekeeping Experiment Station, and is therefore thoroughly tested and does not contain any superfluous items.

Articles grouped near stove:

1 patent gas lighter	$ .25
3 handi-hook pot covers, 9″, 9½″ and 10″	.66
1 8-inch cast iron frying pan	.75
1 5-inch aluminum frying pan	.75
2 dripping pans 9¾ by 14	.40
2 stove cloths	.10
Aluminum griddle, 7¼ inch, for table use	.60
Waffle iron	1.00
Best make of cake turner	.25
	$4.76

Cleaning outfit, grouped near sink:

Ammonia, sal soda solution, etc.
Scouring soap.
Corn-meal and glycerine and alcohol lotion for hands.

Grouped near sink:

Wooden rack or rubber mat to protect sink........$ .75
Dish drainer and pan — 20 inches square 1.50
Dish pan, oval 19 inches long .... .75
1 agate hand basin, suspended at right of sink .... .20
1 agate soap dish .... .15
Agate sink strainer .... .25
Soap shaker .... .18
Dish mop .... .05
Wire dish mop .... .25
2 vegetable brushes with handle, screw eye fastened
    in each handle .... .25
1 milk bottle brush .... .25
Aluminum funnel .... .10
Heart scraper for agate and iron pots and pans.... .10
Rubber plate scraper .... .10
1 crank egg beater .... .18
3 ft. inch. rubber tubing, to fill steamer .... .30
1 small agate stew-pan, capacity 1¼ cups.......... .15
1 small aluminum stew-pan, capacity 1 pt.......... .15
1 2-qt. aluminum shallow stew-pan .... .80
1 3-qt. aluminum shallow stew-pan .... .90
1 4-qt. aluminum shallow stew-pan 1.15
1 5-qt. aluminum shallow stew-pan 1.25

$9.76

Usually grouped on shelf above sink:

Pitchers 1 2-qt., 1 1½-qt., 1 1-qt., 3 small ones.....$1.25
3 meas. cups .... .15
Coffee percolator 2 or 3 pt. size.................. 3.25
Coffee canister (part of stove outfit)
Tea pot .... .25
Tea canister (part of stove outfit)
2 strainers, 15 and 25 cents, total .... .40
Steamer, special type for vegetables and cereal.... 1.19
Steamer, special type of larger size 2.39

· $8.88

Articles to put food away in (also serve as baking dishes):

3 small agate dishes, capacity 1½ pts. ....$ .30
2 agate dishes, capacity 1½ qts. .... .30
3 agate dishes, capacity 2 qts. .... .75
5 qt. agate Berlin kettle .... .50
5 agate ware kitchen plates .... .75
4 small oval dishes at .10 .... .40

$3.00

Built-in, open-shelf kitchen cabinet and equipment,
    or manufactured one selling at $27.50

Cutlery drawer and contents:

Knife box ....$ .25
2 spec. make veg. knives .... .50
2 wooden spoons .... .20
1 spatula .... .25
1 chemists' spatula................................ .20
1 cork screw .... .25
1 can opener .... .25
3 kitchen forks at 20 cents .... .60
3 kitchen knives .... .60
6 German silver table-spoons 1.50
1 doz. teaspoons 1.00
1 perforated cake spoon .... .10
1 egg whip .... .10
Apple corer .... .10
Carving knife .... .75
Sharpening steel .... .25

$6.90

Small articles hanging from shelves:

Set aluminum measuring spoons ....$ .25
Crank egg beater .... .18
2 meas. cups .... .20
Assorted biscuit and doughnut cutters .... .40
1 grater .... .25
1 rack for baking potatoes .... .10
1 nutmeg grater .... .05
Grease brush .... .15

$1.58

Cooking dishes group near cabinet:

4 ~~small white bowls~~	$ .44
2 ~~large yellow mixing~~ bowls	.40
~~Bread mixer~~	1.75
Scales	1.25
Qt. can liquid shortening	.39
~~Cake mix~~er	1.50
~~3 layer cake tins, patent~~ kind	.30
1 round cake tin with funnel	.35
~~2 muffin tins~~ — 12 holes each at 20 cents each	.40
1 loaf tin	.25
Pastry board	.30
Magic cover when rolling out pastry	.65
~~Rolling pin~~	.25
~~3 pie plates, 9 in. diam.~~	.30
~~3 pie plates, shallow 9½~~	.30
~~Lemon squeezer~~	.10

$8.93

Salad outfit:

Salad basket containing
Garlic coves, paprika.
Salt and pepper shakers.
Small bottle tarragon vinegar.
Cost of outfitting $1.00

Miscellaneous:

Coffee mill	$ .75
Porcelain salt box	.25
Clock, octagonal 8-day	3.00
Scrap basket	.60
Scissors	.25
Kitchen stool	1.50
1 meat saw, 14-inch	.75
Vegetable slicer	.75
Thermometer, chemists' tested thermometer	6.00
~~2 Russia~~ iron biscuit sheets, 17 inches square	2.00
Puree strainer	2.00
~~1 strawberry huller~~	.10
Iron kettle for deep fat frying	.75
Frying basket with handle	.45

$19.15

Special place provided for:

2 shelf steamer	$4.50
Meat grinder	1.25
Chopping bowl and knife	.45
Egg poacher	.60
Large tea-pot for company use	.50
2 small crocks for eggs, etc., at 20 cents each......	.40
2 small jelly moulds at 15 cents each	.30
	$8.00

Ice cream freezer, 2-qt.	$1.85
Ice pick	.30
Ice mallet	.30
Canvas bag for cracking ice	.15
	$2.60

Refrigerator, best make porcelain enamel lined,
rear or end icing door, ice capacity 125 lbs.....$54.00

Kitchen linen outfit:

1 doz. kitchen towels, loose mesh crash	$1.20
1 doz. linen tea-towels	2.40
6 dish cloths	.25
1 roll of paper toweling, put up near sink..........	1.50
2 lettuce bags of cheese cloth	.20
1 doz. hemmed cheese cloth squares for straining jelly and fat	.25
	$5.80

Kitchen cleaning outfit:

1 self-wringing mop	$1.50
1 broom, dust-pan and brush	1.00
2 outing flannel floor cloths	.20
1 flannel stove-cloth — old underwear or of new material	.10
½ doz. old soft cloths for cleaning, hemmed and marked	.25
	$3.05

The total cost of a liberal outfit for kitchen where

stove, sink and hot water heating systems are furnished by the landlord is therefore seen to be $163.91. (Groups 1 to 15 inclusive.)   Where the cost of stove, sink and hot water heating systems must also be included in the estimate and the kitchen must be heated by an extra radiator from the furnace they will cost as follows:

Stove and fireless cooker, best make of each, combined or separate ....$	64.00
Hot water radiator and grill	18.00
Hot water heating system with jacket to boiler...	31.50
Sink, wall-type white enameled with one drainboard	37.50
Equipment, groups 1 to 15 inclusive	163.91
	$314.91

SUMMARY

Cost of furnishing a rented kitchen, where stove, sink, etc., are furnished by landlord:

Least expensive outfit — see page 137, from $35.14 to ....$	67.89
Liberal outfit	163.91

Cost of furnishing kitchen where stove, sink, etc., must also be included in estimate:

Least expensive outfit, see page 137 ....$	126.54
Liberal outfit	314.91

OUTFIT FOR FAMILY OF TWO

The great difference in selecting equipment for a family of two instead of for a family of five or six is found to be in the choice of smaller sizes of stew-pans, baking-dishes, coffee percolator, tea-pot, etc. If a family of two expect to keep up the variety and standard of living of a larger family and to entertain frequently, very much the same outfit should be purchased as for the larger family, substituting a small size of these special dishes for the larger size given on the list. It is possible, however, for young people to get along in great comfort with the " light housekeeping equipment " and postpone for some time the more serious responsibility of keeping house. It is almost play with the right equipment and carefully chosen menus to set a table for two people, whereas a more formal living is nearly as much work for two as it is for six or ten. We therefore refer young housekeepers to the chapter on " Light Housekeeping," and advise them to begin with this outfit, adding to it the other things later on.

X

TIME AND LABOR-SAVING EQUIPMENT

THE fireless cooker should be named first among the modern inventions calculated to economize the time and energy of the home-maker. While it has been heralded chiefly as a fuel-saver, its possibilities are even greater in the direction of conservation of woman's labor. This type of cooking is, indeed, the most satisfactory, economical, efficient method of cooking known. It is amazing that there should be so little accurate information on the subject, and that so few accurate recipes should have been given out. No thoroughly satisfactory book on fireless cooking has yet been published. The housekeeper is advised to select the best make of fireless cook stove that she can get, and devote as much time as she can to the study of its possibilities.

Most housekeepers are now aware that fireless cooking is based on the principle of utilizing conserved heat. The viands to be prepared, ragouts, for instance, or casserole dishes, are brought to the boiling point on the gas stove in a specially constructed fireless cooker utensil. The utensil fits into a corresponding well in an air-tight, insulated box where the cooling is so prolonged as to amount, virtually, to a cooking process. The process may be intensified to any degree by means of heated iron or soap-stone discs called radiators, which are enclosed in the well with the utensil, and serve to maintain as high a temperature as any given process may require.

So much of the success of fireless cooking is dependent upon having exact temperature records for heating the radiators, that it is advisable to purchase a special thermometer for this use. Exact temperatures can then be added to recipes, and the time of cooking noted. This data will serve as a reliable guide the next time the same dish is prepared.

When the radiators are heated on a gas stove, waste of gas may be prevented by placing an agate plate above the radiating disc while it is being heated, thus covering in and conserving the heat. Radiators not in use should be kept warm on the steam radiator grill or the back of the kitchen stove. In summer they will store up a high degree of heat by merely being placed in the sun. Keeping them partially warm will markedly lessen the length of time required to heat them.

All slow-cooking processes can be carried on in the fireless cooker at a minimum of expense. The initial expense is only the fuel necessary to heat the radiators, and the ten or fifteen minutes' cooking required to bring the food to the boiling point.

As a time-saver the method has advantages even
more important.

Every woman knows that there are two things
that make cooking tedious and confining. First
the waiting around for things to cook after the
actual work of preparation has been done, as in
" watching up " the cooking of pot-roasts, stews,
etc. Second the necessity of cooking at an inconvenient time in order to economize fuel. This is

Fig. 28.— The large utensil is an aluminum double boiler inset for fireless cooker well. The stew pans represented
are the most efficient shape for conserving fuel.

always a problem with a coal range, and must be
carefully considered in the use of a gas oven.

From the point of view of conserving the housekeeper's time, the most economical way of working
is to do things of the same general kind at the same
time. With the fireless cooker this is made possible. After the breakfast dishes are washed, the
noon meal can be prepared, put in the fireless
cooker, and so timed that it will be ready to put
on the table without further attention. The house-

keeper is then free until luncheon to use her time advantageously in some other part of the house except the kitchen. In the same way dinner can be prepared while lunch is being cleared away, and the afternoon is left free for errands, calls or a walk in the open air. The breakfast cereal can be cooked while one is doing up the supper dishes, and may be left in the cooker to cook itself over-night. (Double boiler inset for cereal cooking, Fig. 28.)

Foods, whether hot or cold, can be kept for hours at an even temperature in the well of the fireless cooker. In the case of hot viands there is no danger of food drying up as long as there is enough moisture in the food compartment to preserve the atmosphere of steam. The radiators should not be too hot. In fact, unless the food is to be left for three or four hours or more, the radiators need not be used at all. One hole of the fireless cooker may be used for hot dishes, another for ice-cream or frozen pudding. Iced dishes will keep quite as well in the fireless cooker as in a freezer if properly packed in ice.

The fireless cooker may also be used for raising bread. The well is brought to a temperature of 70 degrees F. by means of a radiator of the proper temperature. The dough is then placed in the aluminum utensil and is covered and left for the necessary time in the well. A small bread-mixer will fit into an eight-quart well.

In most families it is found to be convenient

to can only a few jars of fruit or vegetables at a time, and in such cases the fireless cooker may be used advantageously in the work of canning and preserving. Often two or three jars may be fitted into a busy morning when a larger quantity would be impossible. Sometimes extra fruit that will not keep may be prepared in the evening and cooked

FIG. 29.—An efficient layer-cake pan which prevents cake from sticking.

over night in the fireless cooker. To can fruit in this way prepare as for other method and pack it in jars. Adjust the rubber and cover, fill the jar completely with hot syrup, and seal at once. Have the fireless cooker utensil heated before jars are placed in it, and cover completely with boiling water. Cover the utensil and set away in cooker over night or until cold.

When food cooked in the fireless cooker is found to have a stale, unpleasant taste, it is because the cooker has not been properly aired. The lids should never be tightly closed when the cooker is not in use, and should be kept open for several hours after each cooking operation.

In purchasing a fireless cooker the following points should be carefully considered:

1. Durable construction. The cooker should have a well-made hardwood or metal cabinet.
2. Perfect insulation, of cork, magnesia, mineral wool or asbestos.
3. The interior lining of food compartments should be durable and easily cleaned. Aluminum or nickeled copper is best for this reason.
4. There should be a vent-valve to let off excess steam while viands are cooking. This makes roasting and browning possible.
5. Cooker utensils should be of pure, seamless aluminum.
6. The best radiators are of soap-stone, as this retains heat longest.
7. Lever lock should be absolutely tight to prevent loss of steam.
8. There should be stop-hinges to prevent lids from going too far backward.

A good size for the average family is a cooker having one eight-quart and one four-quart well. This size, in the best makes, costs about $16.00.

The equipment of utensils, heating-stones or radiators, racks and covers that go with the fireless cooker should all be kept near the place where the cooker stands. The best way to provide for this is to have a stand on which the cooker may rest, which is at the same time a cabinet to hold the utensils. The manufactured cabinets have a lower compartment with two doors, a sliding shelf and a lower drawer.   These cabinets are equipped with good castors so that the whole cooker outfit may be moved about easily.   Cabinets large enough for a two-hole cooker cost about $7.25.

A very serviceable cabinet may be made at home by using ordinary wood and staining it to match the cooker.   Such a home-made stand is shown in the illustration facing page 44.   A smaller one can be made of lumber found in the house and at a cost, with the castors, of $1.50.   The open shelves are quite as convenient as those closed in with doors.

There are many advantages of the fireless cooker outside of the most obvious function, the saving of fuel, time and energy.   Among these may be noted the following:

1. The cooking of food in a tightly sealed vessel, from which no odors or steam can escape, preserves as nothing else can, the flavor of meats and vegetables.

2. Food which absorbs water easily, and therefore scorches unless carefully watched, can be cooked in the fireless cooker without any danger.

3. Fireless cooking, when thoroughly mastered, gives more uniform results than any other method.

COOKING BY STEAM

Great economy of time and strength can be effected by means of steam cooking.   We are so used to baking, boiling and frying our food that it seems almost revolutionary to suggest a simpler method. There is, it is true, a limited amount of steam cooking done in almost every home. We all have steamed brown bread, and once in a while a steamed pudding. But the use of steam as a resource for preparing all kinds of food is almost unknown.

The greatest advantage of cooking by steam lies in the fact that it conserves in the food all the delicate flavors and mineral salts which are lost in boiling, and gives us a wholesome, delicious fare with a minimum of effort, expense and work. The possibilities of steam for this use were first brought to the attention of the public in the writings of Mr. Charles Barnard, the founder of the Housekeeping Experiment Station. While steam cooking has been practised in some form or other for unknown years, it still remained a practically undeveloped resource until he convinced progressive housekeepers of its value. All kinds of vegetables and fruits are delicious when prepared in this way. One may have steamed potatoes, rice, apples, cabbage, tomatoes, corn, etc. Vegetables with a strong taste should first be parboiled for ten minutes in boiling water, and then put in the steamer to finish. Several dishes may be prepared at one time in the steamer and the flavors will not mingle. Food may be placed directly in the dishes in which it is to appear on the table, thus saving dish-washing. A whole meal may be prepared over one burner, thus reducing the cost of fuel to a minimum.

Steamed food requires no watching while it is cooking if the proper amount of water is placed in the water pan. The water pan must of course be kept from getting dry, and a little experience is needed to know just how long each type of steamer can be safely left without attention. In homes where meals cannot be served at regular times

Fig. 30.— Simplest type of steamer. Illustrations intended to show perforations in upper pan. One of the most valuable kitchen utensils.

steaming and fireless cooking are the only methods that can be employed without spoiling the food and ruining the disposition of the cook.

Three types of steamer are illustrated. The simplest form (see Fig. 30) is suited to any family because it may be used for a variety of purposes. It will be the only steamer needed for a family of two, where a fireless cooker is also used. But if there is no fireless cooker it will be best to buy the small steamer and a two-shelf one also.

The two-or-three-shelf steamer with copper bottom (see Fig. 31) is ideal for a family of four or less, as it will hold enough for an entire meal. For larger families either a four-compartment cooker of this type is recommended, or the round type (see Fig. 32) of separate sections. This type has some advantages over the square type, because its parts are removable and one can use one section, or two, or three.

Care must be taken to wipe out the cookers after

FIG. 31.— Steamers with two or more compartments are economical of fuel and labor.

FIG. 32.— Steamer having separate sections.

use. No water should be allowed to stand in them. If it is poured out immediately and the cooker is dried over a warm radiator it will keep in good condition for several years.

The awkward business of filling a steam cooker can be accomplished with ease if a small piece of rubber tubing is kept near the sink. Connect one end with the faucet and let the water run into the bottom of the steamer.

Certain vegetables, such as potatoes, are better if allowed to rest on a perforated plate while steaming, so that they do not rest in the water of condensation, which collects on the bottom of the vessel. Potatoes are more delicious cooked in this than in any other way.

WHEEL CARTS AND WHEELED SERVING TABLES

Some form of serving table on wheels is an indispensable adjunct to the efficient home. As a means of conserving time and energy it almost ranks with the business man's automobile.

Its greatest usefulness is found in homes where there are no servants, or in large families where only one maid is kept. Its office at meal-time is practically that of a substitute for the labors of a second girl. It is first moved to the china closet and buffet and receives its load of dishes, cutlery and linen for setting the table. It is then wheeled to a convenient position, and the things for the table are unloaded and put in their proper places. Those that need to be warmed are taken to the kitchen or the hot grill in pantry or dining-room. The serving dishes go out to the warming-oven in the kitchen. The table is now empty and in convenient position to receive the food from pantry and kitchen. Bread and butter, milk, water, etc., are first placed on the lower shelf of the wheel cart, together with a reserve of uncut bread, the crumbing outfit and a plate scraper. Next the dessert and dessert plates are placed on this shelf. If the dessert needs to be kept hot it may either be placed over a water pan of boiling water, or kept warm on a little table stove which stands on the cart. Thermos bottles are very useful for hot or cold sauces or for hot or cold drinks. There should be two of these for comfort. Last of all the food is dished up and placed on the top of the table. The cart is then wheeled to the dining-room or out-door breakfast room, and the first course is served. If soup or some relish precedes the meat and vegetable course, these must be kept warm in the meantime. Nickel meat platters with covers are indispensable for this need. (Fig. 35.) After each course is finished the dishes are passed to the hostess, who places them on the wheel cart, which is always at her left. Before the dessert, crumbs are removed by passing the crumb tray to each person in turn. After dessert coffee is made at the table or on a little table stove.

When the meal is over the dishes are piled on the wheel cart. Table linen, condiment sets, etc., are put where they belong. The dishes, carefully scraped, are wheeled out on the cart to the sink, where they remain ready for washing.

This procedure, with such variation as circumstances require, may be worked out to satisfactorily meet the needs of the average family. But special thought and some additional equipment are necessary if the family is large, or if elaborate meals are served. The general tendency is toward simplified living; and for such conditions the serving

Reprinted courtesy of "The Outlook"

Remodelled kitchen, Stamford, Conn. Note concentration of working processes by grouping of sink, range and pastry table. Wheel tray near sink

table is fully adequate, and the greatest possible comfort.

LABOR-SAVING AND FUEL-SAVING UTENSILS

The following list of labor-saving and fuel-saving utensils should be included in every kitchen outfit. The housekeeper with the least money to spend needs the help and saving in strength even more than the one with ample income. If there is very little baking of bread, cake or muffins, the bread and cake mixers may be omitted:

Labor-Saving Equipment.

Coffee Percolator ...$3.25
Bread Mixer 1.75

Cake Mixer 1.50

Potato Ricer .... .35

Meat Chopper 1.25
Slaw Cutter .... .35

Puree Strainer 2.00

Electric Iron 5.00

Dish Drainer 1.50
Plate Scraper .... .10

Fuel-Saving Equipment.

Fireless Cooker. (One with two compartments is recommended for average needs. A single compartment, 8-qt. well, will however, do excellent service.)

Steamers. (One small one of specially convenient type is a necessity. A two-shelf or four-shelf steamer in addition will prepare several dishes at the same time.)

Small Toaster to use over one gas burner.

The following labor savers are extremely convenient, but are not necessities in all families:

Mayonnaise Mixer ..$1.25
Bread Slicer .... .75
Pastry Bag and Outfit 2.25
Rosette Irons ...... .75
Cream Whip 1.00
Grater for Fresh Corn .25

Apple Parer from .75
  to $1.25
Cherry Stoner ...... .75
Ham Saw .... .75
Saratoga Parer and
  Slicer .... .25

Grape Fruit Knife .. .50   Butter Ball Pats .... .44
Pineapple Snips ..... .25

DESIRABLE DINING-ROOM EQUIPMENT

The new housekeeping has transformed dining-room as well as kitchen equipment. Housekeepers

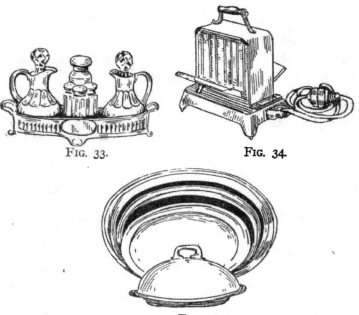

FIG. 33.   FIG. 34.

FIG. 35.

When cooking is done in the dining-room the equipment must be dainty as well as efficient. The condiment set (FIG. 33), electric toaster (FIG. 34) and nickel platters (FIG. 35) illustrate a few desirable pieces.

doing their own work spend less on expensive china, cut glass and table linen, and in its place buy the attractive outfit of dining-room equipment enumerated below:

Wheel Cart ....
  from $5.50 to..... $18.00
Turn Table or Lazy
  Susan 10.00
Electric Toaster 5.00
Nickel Baking Dish,
  pottery lined 3.20
Silver Meat Dish, 10-
  in. 5.40
Nickel Cover to fit.. 3.35

6 inch Electric Table
  Stove .... $ 7.50
Electric Blazing Dish 2.50
Or Alcohol Stove and
  Chafing Dish 10.50
Mahoganite Tray, 25-
  in. 8.00
Condiment Sets 6.00
Thermos Bottles, 1
  pt. size $2.50, qt.. 3.50
Carved Bread Board .75

TIME-SAVING EQUIPMENT EVERY KITCHEN SHOULD HAVE

Clock.
Scrap Basket.
Supply of Pins in tin box or cushion.
Steel Skewers.
Refined Cotton Seed Oil in Quart Can. (This liquid shortening saves time and dish-washing in all recipes which require melted shortening.)

Absorbent Cotton in Covered Jar. (Should be kept on hand, as a thin layer is useful under coffee in Percolator when coffee is ground too fine.)
Soft-Haired Paint Brush, 1-in. wide. (For use in greasing Pans, top of bread, rolls, etc.)
Pad and Pencil for Jotting down Kitchen needs. (Best size called Telephone Pads.)

SMALL KITCHEN NECESSITIES

Bag for brown paper made of denim or ticking, size 16 by 26 inches or larger, made with a loop in upper left-hand corner and hung on a hook in closet or pantry to hold empty paper bags, brown paper, newspapers, etc.

Small bag or box for twine.

Handy jar, containing cup-hooks, screw-eyes, etc., so that each new addition to kitchen equipment may be hung at once in place.

Two nails hung together by wire and suspended from hook. Useful to punch holes in sifting top cans, olive oil cans, etc.

Small hammer.

Labels, convenient size for kitchen use.

Darning needle and strong twine for sewing up stuffed fish, fowl, shoulder of lamb, etc.

Non-rustable pot-covers, either aluminum or agate-ware, or handi-hook type. If the former, a rack near stove to keep them in, to save steps in getting them and returning them to their place. If paper roll is near they can be wiped at once after use and returned to their place.

SMALL KITCHEN CONVENIENCES

Heart scraper of aluminum for scraping agate or iron ware dishes.

Funnel.

Dish-protector to go on faucet and prevent breakage of china.

Corks, assorted sizes, for use as stoppers. Also a supply of large corks for cleaning kitchen knives.

Sterilized baking testers.

Scissors. As necessary to a complete kitchen as a frying pan. Among the uses they serve are the following:

Cutting raisins or figs.

Cutting center from grape-fruit.

Cutting lettuce, parsley, etc., for garnishing.

Cutting thin sandwiches in fancy shapes, oblongs, squares, rounds, etc.

Cutting the joint of a chicken.
Cutting angelica to decorate fancy cakes.
Cutting twine and paper.
Cutting clams for chowder.
Dicing bacon and salt pork.

OUTFIT OF PAPER FOR KITCHEN

Flat package of tissue paper for greasing pans, etc. Should be kept in a handy place near work-table.

Newspaper cut in quarters and kept in bag or drawer in kitchen to be used, to protect kitchen table whenever dirty work has to be done.

Paper towelling or absorbent paper to replace roller towel. Also valuable to absorb superfluous grease from croquettes, fried mush, doughnuts, etc.

Oiled paper saved from bread or bought in rolls at 5 and 10 cent store to wrap up sandwiches, cheese, meat, etc.

Paper Bags. Either regular cooking bags, or bags saved from groceries. Useful for warming up muffins, rolls or biscuits. Place muffins, etc., in bag. Sprinkle lightly with water, tie up end and put in oven for 5 to 10 minutes. The enclosed steam makes them like new.

UTENSILS THAT SERVE A DOUBLE PURPOSE

One of the greatest benefits that is coming to the kitchen from an intelligent study on the part of the manufacturer, of the housekeeper's needs is the development of utensils that save unnecessary equipment. These may serve double purposes and at the same time conserve fuel. Such a development is the tea-kettle of aluminum with double boiler inset; the double boiler inset (see Fig. 28) to the aluminum fireless cooker utensils; the triple nesting compartments fitting into one hole of the fireless cooker; and a food strainer which may serve in turn as a steamer or a colander. All of these utensils are very valuable additions to the kitchen outfit. There are also on the market a number that are said to serve many purposes but that do not serve any one really well. The housekeeper must be on her guard to buy only articles of known merit.

XI

LIGHT HOUSEKEEPING EQUIPMENT

THE great improvement in kitchen and dining-room conveniences has made it possible for any small sized family to keep house comfortably with a very simple outfit. When we eliminate from the regular work of the kitchen the cake and bread making, the making of pies, deep-fat frying and all canning and preserving, we find that the number of utensils needed is cut in half. We find that with a few well chosen, efficient tools we can get up very attractive meals, that we can enjoy almost as much freedom as in boarding and far more home comfort.

The three essentials of light housekeeping are the fireless cooker, steamer and chafing dish. Therefore these three articles must head the list of any light housekeeping equipment. If you want to do a little muffin making or cake baking, you must learn to bake in the fireless cooker. An occasional roast, also, may come from the fireless cooker. If you want to save time and avoid unnecessary dishwashing, you must learn serving-dish cookery, placing your food in the dishes in which they are to appear on the table, and doing the cooking in the steamer. Not only will you be delighted with the ease of work done in this way, but you will wonder at the delicious flavors that are brought out in the food. If you want to have jolly little informal suppers and invite in four or five friends, you will find your little outfit adequate for delightful chafing dish spreads.

A very tiny kitchenette is all that is needed for light housekeeping. Sometimes a big closet or pantry in old fashioned city houses can be utilized in this way. It ought to have good light and good ventilation. There are ingenious ways of securing ventilation; but at least one window opening outdoors is an essential. If your alcove or closet does not afford that, you had better have your stove and work table in the living-room. They can be enclosed in sightly wooden cabinets that close up to look like a desk or other article of sitting-room furniture, when the contents are not in use. The closet can then be utilized for storage of supplies and for dish-washing. With the addition of a good zinc-covered table an ordinary stationary lavatory will answer this purpose very well. Nothing is needed except that it be sanitary and that it enable you to get rid of the waste water.

However arranged, the light housekeeping equipment should include a drawer for cutlery; a drawer for table-linen (together with outfits of paper napkins, table-cloths and doilies). There should be a convenient place for minute supplies of flour, salt, pepper, sugar, etc., so that everything you need for your play housekeeping is right at hand, just as it is in the more formal kitchen. Your tiny ice chest must keep fresh milk, butter, cream and salad materials always ready for use.

Any one carrying out this plan in the city has the choice, in most houses or apartments, of three fuels, gas, alcohol or electricity. The latter would be preferable because it is the most convenient, and because it does not exhaust the oxygen in the air. But except for the lightest of light housekeeping, it would be found more expensive than the others. Gas, where it can be had, is at present prices the most practical, and alcohol next. The equipment for either gas or alcohol is practically the same, except for the stove. For electric cooking a special outfit is desirable, because in order to economize fuel the cooking utensils must clamp fast to the electric stove. Moreover, special care must be taken in wiring to have the voltage right for the utensils that are to be used.

You will notice that, in the list that follows, a dozen and a half plates, a dozen cups and saucers and a dozen glasses are included, while the rest of the outfit is limited to six pieces. This is to allow for entertaining. A good deal of simple but delightful hospitality is possible if one has cups and saucers, glasses and plates enough. For formal entertaining and especially elaborate dinners the light housekeeper must go to a restaurant.

REGULAR LIGHT HOUSEKEEPING OUTFIT

Two-burner Junior gas stove (See Figs. 20 and 12) and single alcohol stove for table use ....$	4.50
Or, two-burner alcohol stove and single alcohol stove for table use	10.50
Home-made cabinet for stove to rest on	3.50
Fireless cooker with one 4-qt. and one 8-qt. well, aluminum lined	16.00
Fireless cooker cabinet with shelves for utensils ..	2.50
Single steamer of agate ware (to be kept under shelf of stove cabinet) (See Fig. 30)	1.19
Two-shelf steamer (to be kept under shelf of stove cabinet) (See Fig. 31)	4.50
Chafing dish	10.00
Coffee percolator, three pints....................	3.50
Wheel cart, oak or mahogany, $20.00; plain wood..	• 5.50
Small cabinet with bins underneath and pastry boards to pull out	6.00
Stool, a comfortable height for the worker	1.50
Chest refrigerator	13.00
	$82.19

Dish pan ....$	.50	Amount forward.$	3.33
Soap shaker	.18	Two measuring cups.	.10
Dish mop	.10	Extension strainer ...	.35
Vegetable brush	.05	Small strainer	.10
Vegetable knife......	.15	Flour sifter	.25
Bread knife	.50	One small stew pan ..	.15
Tin funnel	.05	One aluminum cover .	.15
Two wooden spoons..	.20	5 inch frying pan	.50
Four aluminum tea-spoons	.20	4 small white bowls .	.44
		4 agate dishes	.60
Two plated table-spoons	.50	4 agate plates	.60
		4 agate cups	.60
Kitchen knives and forks	.40	Lemon squeezer	.10
		Egg beater	.25
Cork screw	.25		
Can opener	.25		$7.52
	$3.33		

Amount forward ....$ 7.52
Double cake closet with five compartments for crack-
    ers, cookies, cake, pie and bread 4.50
One-half dozen pint jars to hold small supplies.... .45
One-half dozen quart jars to hold small supplies.. .45
Pitchers: Qt. size, pt., half-pt., and 3 small...... .80

                                                                      $13.72

DINING-ROOM OUTFIT FOR LIGHT HOUSE-KEEPING

6 plated tea-spoons ....$ .60
4 plated table-spoons 1.00
6 plated forks 1.50
6 plated knives 1.50
4 plated dessert spoons 1.00
Carved bread board 1.00
Sugar bowl .... .25
Teapot .... .25
1 dozen cups and saucers 2.40
6 Sauce dishes .... .60
1 dozen bread and butter plates 1.20
18 Supper plates 1.80
6 Dinner plates .... .60
2 Open vegetable dishes .... .60
2 Platters .... .80
1 dozen tumblers 1.20
Silver carving knife and fork 5.00
Electric toaster 5.00

                                          $26.30

2 Lunch cloths, 1½ yd. size $3.00
1 Doz. napkins, linen. 2.00
4 Doz. crepe paper napkins .... .50
Assorted paper doilies 1.50
Roll paper toweling.. 1.50
2 rolls oiled paper ... .10
Supply of old news-papers.

        $8.60

2 Dustless dustcloths.$ .50
4 Loose woven wash cloths .... .20
2 Flannelette floor cloths .... .40
½ Doz. crash towels. .60
½ Doz. linen tea tow-els 1.50
Dust-pan, brush and broom 1.00

        $4.20

TOTAL COST OF REGULAR LIGHT HOUSEKEEPING
OUTFIT

Stoves, cookers and special utensils ....$ 82.19
Cooking dishes and small utensils 13.72
Dining-room outfit 26.30
Linen and paper outfit 8.60
Cleaning outfit 4.20

$135.01

LIGHTEST OF ALL OUTFITS

Where only breakfasts are prepared at home, or
for emergency use anywhere, the following list of
light housekeeping utensils will be found exceedingly useful and valuable:

Small alcohol stove (See Size 12) $1.50
4-inch aluminum frying pan .... .30
3-inch aluminum stew-pan with cover .... .40
Nickel tray 1.25
Extension strainer .... .35
Pint bottle of alcohol .... .30
2 cups and saucers .... .50
4 plates .... .40
12 tea-spoons, 4 knives and 4 forks 3.00
Sugar bowl .... .25
Tea canister and small tea-pot .... .25
Cork screw and can opener .... .50
Egg beater .... .18

$9.18

Any one who has never tried it will be amazed
to find how much can be accomplished with the
simple little outfit given above. A shelf or small
closet so fitted up would be found an immense comfort in emergencies in any home. With it people
living in furnished rooms can easily get breakfasts
and occasional suppers. Empty boxes and a pail

or two will enable one to store the small supply of rolls, bread, butter, etc., that one needs to keep on hand for daily use. This same outfit, with some slight modifications, was carried by the author on a walking trip of three days. We omitted the nickel tray, replaced the silver-plated cutlery by kitchen knives, forks and spoons, and the crockery dishes by agate ware. We found the equipment light and compact and fully adequate for breakfasts and suppers. There are few places in these days where one may not easily get good home-made bread and butter, rolls, milk, fresh eggs, etc. So it is possible, with a few well-chosen utensils for cooking, to be very independent.

XII

Disposal of Kitchen Waste

ONE of the most troublesome problems of housekeeping is the proper disposal of garbage. Where the income is liberal and gas is available, a recent invention has completely solved this difficulty.

The garbage is burned in a gas-fired destroyer of excellent design. The destroyer is usually placed beside the kitchen range, and connected with the same flue. It is so well designed that no unpleasant odors escape and the gas burners are so powerful that even green vegetable garbage is reduced to ashes in a short time. The ashes can then be removed from the receiver in the lower part of the destroyer and thrown into the usual garbage can. Ordinarily it takes an hour to an hour and a half to burn up the amount the destroyer will contain. In a small family garbage can be put into the destroyer for several days till it is full, and then burned. No unpleasant odors will escape into the kitchen. The price of the household size is $85.00. The high price makes is prohibitory for the average family, unless several families near together own and use it coöperatively. The garbage can be collected and burned each evening.

A less expensive type of gas garbage burner has satisfactorily stood a nine months' test. It must be installed with a copper stove-pipe instead of an iron one as the gases formed by combustion cause the iron pipe to disintegrate. This type costs $14.00. It will undoubtedly pay in the long run to buy the expensive type, as the former is especially constructed to withstand the intense heat necessary to reduce the garbage to ashes, and also to withstand the corroding action of the gases given out in the process.

The collection of garbage is a problem that ought to be worked out coöperatively in every small town or city, where the work is not undertaken by the public authorities. Even where garbage is collected twice a week, there will be some annoyance from decaying food. In the vicinity of Boston special garbage bags have been made which fit the ordinary garbage can. The bag is placed in the empty can and the garbage put into it. When the can is ready to empty the bag is removed with the garbage and the can is left clean.

CARE OF GARBAGE IN THE COUNTRY

Every householder ought to have a strong galvanized garbage can. The best have wooden supports on the sides to prevent the sides of the can from becoming bent in handling. Such a can costs $3.50. Where the city authorities do not require separate cans for the ashes and garbage, one can

will suffice for most families. An agate-ware pail
can be used instead of the can. The pail should be
kept in a box having a hinged cover. It is not
necessary for the box to have a bottom; it is even
a very good plan to sink the box in the ground.
Sometimes the box is placed against the back wall
of the house and painted the same color. This
makes it neat and inconspicuous. The cover is a

FIG. 36.— Illustrates two views of under-ground garbage can.
The figure at the right shows it before placed in position.
The one at the left after it has been buried in the ground.

necessity, both for sanitary reasons and also to
prevent cats and dogs from getting into the pail
and tipping it over.

Another excellent plan is to install one of the
garbage receivers designed to be sunk in the ground.
(See Fig 36.) The receiver is made of cast iron,
the size of the usual garbage can, with a hinged top.
The iron receiver with its cover is sunk in the earth
near the back door. The regular garbage can is

placed inside the receiver. One container of this type has the cover so made that it can be opened with the foot when the garbage is dumped in. This saves the necessity of setting the garbage down in order to open the cover. The price of this style of container is $12.75 to $21.00, according to size.

It is a good plan to discourage keeping a garbage pail in the kitchen. This plan is often far from sanitary, and the garbage itself draws flies. It is better to make an iron-clad rule that no garbage be kept in the kitchen, and that it be taken out after each meal. Drain the scrapings from the plates and other waste food in the sink drainer, then wrap it up in a newspaper and place it in the covered pail at the back entrance. Paper bags in which groceries come may be saved for this purpose. See that the garbage pail is rinsed out with hot soda solution once a week in winter and two or three times a week in summer.

In country homes, where all kinds of waste must be disposed of by the householder, it is a good plan to keep two extra waste barrels in the cellar. One is used for empty cans, bottles, etc., the other is for waste paper, dust and other dry refuse. All empty cans should be rinsed under the hot water faucet and dried out on the radiator or back of the range before being put in the barrel to prevent unpleasant odors. Arrangements can be made several times a year to have someone call and take the contents of this barrel to the public dump. The contents of the waste paper barrel should be burned in the furnace at convenient times during the week, so as not to affect its running. In summer it may be burned in a wire refuse burner especially sold for the purpose. In the winter, garbage may be burned in the furnace. Often it is buried in the garden or placed in a trench made for the purpose and covered each time with a layer of earth. Where there is an ample garden this is the best method in the long run, though it requires a few more steps.

If garbage is properly drained and wrapped in paper it can be kept in the covered agate pail at the back of the house. Once a day the pail can be emptied in the garden. Scald out the pail often with a strong solution of sal-soda. Where there are coal or wood ranges, much of the light waste can be burned up in the range. The chief cause of unsightly back yards is failure to plan intelligently for the care and disposal of these various kinds of waste. If families would coöperate in this matter the individual housekeeper would be saved much annoying work.

XIII

DISH-WASHING AND DAILY CARE OF KITCHEN

ANY operation that has to be repeated three times a day is an important one to reduce to its simplest elements so that it can be done in the least time, without haste or sense of weariness in its accomplishment. By most women dish-washing is considered by far the most disagreeable of all the home duties. They will therefore welcome suggestions whereby its irksomeness may be mitigated and the time required for its performance cut short.

Dish-washing is one of the few household tasks which has not, thus far, been simplified by any thoroughly practical labor-saving device. Excellent machines for boarding-house and hotel use can be recommended, but the expense of these makes them prohibitive for the home. Moreover, to be practical for home use, a dish-washing machine should be very simply constructed. Otherwise the care of the machine would amount to more each day than the work of dish-washing. However, it is surprising to find how greatly the process may be simplified by a certain amount of system, and the following inexpensive equipment:

Dish-washing Outfit:

Plate scraper	$ .10
Dish mop with handle	.10
Dish pan	.75
Dish cloth	.05
Two linen towels	.36
Dish dryer, 20-inch	1.50
Soap shaker	.18
Dutch Cleanser	.10
Bath brick	.10
	$3.24

In addition to the above equipment, the Wheel Cart, already enumerated in the chapter on Labor Saving Devices, has a most important use in connection with the perennial task of washing dishes, since it saves practically all the laborious work of carrying utensils to and fro. These cost from $5.50 to $20.00. (See frontispiece.)

No part of the household work is done to better advantage by two people working together than is dish-washing. Not only is there a gain in time through coöperation, but all sense of drudgery and weariness is removed. It is a process that need not at all disturb conversation as it becomes almost automatic after it has been performed a number of times.

It begins in the dining-room with clearing the table. Two people remain after the meal is over. One stands on one side of the table and passes the dishes to the other who has the wheel cart on her right. All the dishes being placed within her reach, the housekeeper scrapes each dish with the plate scraper, and piles each size by itself on the cart. The silver is all placed on one empty dish.

The assistant meanwhile gathers up the salt and pepper, napkins, bibs, doilies and any miscellaneous articles that do not go to the kitchen, and puts them away in their proper places. As the housemother wheels the cart out to the kitchen the assistant folds up the table-cloth, runners or doilies and puts them away. If the table-cloth is a long one, the house-mother assists in folding it before going out to the kitchen.

The sink has a drain-board at the left, if there is room for but one drain-board. On it is the dish drainer which is twenty inches square, and has wire supports to hold the dishes. (See frontispiece.)

In our kitchenette at the Housekeeping Experiment Station we are working out the Minimum Space problem, and therefore the single left-hand drain-board is all that is possible. We find it in some ways an advantage. The dishes are handled directly from the wheel cart, instead of being transferred from it to the right-hand drain-board; and thus an extra handling is saved.

The housemother then stands at the sink with the wheel cart at her left. She fills her pan with very hot water, without soap, puts the silver in one end to soak, dips the tumblers in one by one and transfers them to a dish on the wheel cart to be wiped at once. She has just about time to wash and wipe the glasses while the assistant is brushing up crumbs in the dining-room and putting away the food. Next she places the piles of dishes in her dish-pan, being careful not to rest them on the silver which has been left in the pan to soak. Each piece of china is taken up in the left hand, washed with the handle mop held in the right, and placed in the rack on the left-hand drain-board to dry. By this time the china is washed and water is cool enough to plunge the hands in and wash the silver without any discomfort. Next all left-over pots and pans are washed, though these should be few, as cooking dishes ought, as far as possible, to be washed and put away while the preparation of the meal is in progress. Any that have not been so done, or any that needed soaking, are attended to last of all when the dining-room dishes are out of the way. Finally the water is poured out, the dish-pan wiped and hung up, the sink-rack wiped and placed near the radiator to dry. The sink should be wiped out with Dutch Cleanser or Porcela, and flushed thoroughly with very hot water. The dish-cloth and towels should be rinsed in clean water and hung up to dry.

In the meantime the assistant has finished her duties, and has taken the dishes from the rack and given them the necessary wiping, piled them up and put them away. If very hot water is used for washing and rinsing, as is usually the case, most of the dishes dry without any wiping. For a family of five, the entire process does not take more than twenty minutes to half an hour.

The advantage of this method is that it offers an opportunity to the children to work with their mother, giving them valuable training while they are greatly lightening a rather dreary task. Where there are no children it cultivates in grown-ups the habit of burden-sharing and comradeship in the daily tasks, thus transforming the whole atmosphere of the home from one of drudgery to happy coöperation and companionship in work for the common benefit.

CARE OF THE HANDS

After dish-washing or any other kitchen task which is hard on the hands, wash them carefully in Ivory soap suds and corn meal until all the dirt is removed. Then wipe dry and rub a little glycerine lotion on the hands. This keeps the hands soft and white.*

At the Housekeeping Experiment Station we have a white enameled sink, a zinc-covered work-table and aluminum utensils for cooking. This equipment greatly simplifies the dish-washing process. Aluminum ware is kept clean by boiling up the utensils with clear water on the stove. If badly stained the discolorations may be removed by adding one teaspoonful of oxalic acid to the water

* Glycerine lotion consists of equal parts of glycerine and bay rum or glycerine and alcohol. A bottle of this, as well as a small jar of corn meal should be kept on the shelf above the kitchen sink.

and boiling for five to ten minutes. If this is not enough, dip a moist cloth into Dutch Cleanser or Dutch Cleanser and powdered bath-brick, and rub the surface until the stain disappears. Special directions are given elsewhere for precautions in the use of aluminum ware.

In the daily care of the kitchen and its equipment the following cleaning materials will be found extremely valuable. They take up but little space and are convenient in numberless emergencies that continually arise in every household. They are the basis for most of the cleaning preparations widely advertised and selling at high prices:

Denatured alcohol.   Rotten-stone.
Alum.   Salt.
Ammonia.   Separator oil.
Bath-Brick.   Soap.
Black lead (for coal stove Vinegar.
  only.)   Washing soda.
Kerosene.   Floor wax.
Olive oil.   Whiting.

The housekeeper will also need:

An apron of heavy denim   Some Canton flannel.
  or oil-cloth.   Some heavy flannel.
A piece of Brussels carpet. Flannel for waxing.
A chamois skin.   Flannelette for dusters.
A few yards of cheese   Rubber gloves.
  cloth.   A 5 cent mitt for kerosene.
A scrub cloth.   A supply of cotton waste
A soft cloth.   (sold at hardware stores).

The following is a list of necessary cleaning implements and tools:

Bottle brush ....$ .25 Dauber ....$ .25
Cornice brush .....   .50 2 Tin funnels 20

Scrub brush, .15 to..	.25	2 Hand basins	.40
Painters' soft camel's	.	Dry mop or dustless	
hair brush	.75	mop, .60 to	1.50
Radiator brush	.35	Self-wringing mop..	1.50
Vegetable brushes		Old sauce-pan.	
(two)	.10	Step ladder	2.25
Broom	.50	Whisk broom	.25
Long-handled floor		Hammer	.50
brush	1.00	Monkey wrench	1.00
Carpet sweeper, best		Screw driver	.75
grade $4.50, or		Tack puller	.25
Vacuum cleaner, ..			
$5.00 to 135.00			

HOUSEKEEPERS' TOOLS

A handy box of housekeepers' tools and implements can be purchased for $2.50. Or a homemade wooden box with sliding cover can be fitted up at a cost of about $1.50. Seven by 13 inches is a convenient size. It should contain the following outfit:

Long narrow hammer.
Screw driver.
Tack puller.
Awl.
Assorted tacks of the following sizes: one package of each: 12 oz., 8 oz., 6 oz., 4 oz., 3 oz., 2 oz. Also matting tacks, double pointed, japanned and steel, 8 oz. size; assorted 1-in. wire brads, 1-in. wire nails, etc.; box of upholstery tacks; box of assorted screws in sizes from 1-in. down; screw-eyes, 1 doz., each medium and larger size; round and square cup-hooks, 1 doz each.

CARE OF THE SINK

The care of an enamel or porcelain sink is a very simple matter. The bottom should be protected with a wooden rack or rubber mat to protect the surface from scratches. Enamel, if once scratched, cannot be repaired, so it is important to prevent this. After each dish-washing the rack should be removed. The sink should be washed with hot, soapy water, flushed thoroughly with hot water, rinsed and dried. This will remove all odors of strong vegetables, and will keep grease from adhering to the pipes. Where dishes are scraped before washing and all grease is removed from frying pans very little care of the sink drain will be necessary. In the ordinary home, however, grease finds its way in quantities down the sink drain, and a daily application of strong soda is necessary to prevent grease from adhering to the sides of the pipes. Where daily care is exercised this need be done only once a week. Whether daily or weekly, the process of flushing the pipes is as follows:

Make a strong solution of soda, in the proportion of one-third cup of sal soda to one quart of water. Bring to a boil in an old saucepan which may be kept for this work. Stir with a wooden stick which can be burned up afterward. Place a tin funnel in sink plug hole and pour down the quart of boiling soda solution. Be careful not to let the soda get on the hands or drain boards. In half an hour plug the sink, fill with hot water, remove the plug and let the rush of water finish cleaning the trap.

To clean an iron sink daily, pour a small amount of kerosene in the sink and wipe thoroughly with newspaper, which should afterward be burned. The kerosene cuts the grease as nothing else will.

CARE OF FRYING PANS

If grease has not been allowed to burn in the frying pan it may be strained through a cloth or fine wire strainer and used again. If burnt pour in the garbage can. Under no circumstances allow it to go down the sink drain. Wipe the utensil with soft newspaper to remove all grease; then wash, using plenty of soapy water, rinse thoroughly and dry. If the frying pan is of aluminum ware it needs no drying. Iron or tin ware should be dried in the warming oven of a coal range or on the radiator grill in a gas kitchen before being put away. It is a bad practice to dry out wet articles in the oven of a gas stove, as it makes it rust.

Soda solution should never be used on aluminum ware, but is a very good thing for iron. Scouring the inside of iron or steel utensils with any kind of sand-soap or mineral soap makes the surface smooth and bright.

CARE OF ALUMINUM

If aluminum is not used for vegetables with strong acid or when boiling eggs, it will not discolor and needs very little care. Before using any polish fill the utensil with water and bring to a boil on the stove. For bad discolorations add oxalic acid to the water in the proportion of one teaspoonful of acid to two quarts of water. If the stain still remains rub the surface with a damp cloth dipped in whiting or Dutch Cleanser. Black spots made by allowing food to " burn on " can be removed by subjecting the utensil for a minute or two to intense heat in a gas oven. This must be carefully watched, as aluminum will melt if heat is applied too long.

CARE OF BRASS, COPPER OR TIN

Rub the surface first with a cloth dipped in vinegar or lemon juice. Then rub thoroughly with a paste made of rotton-stone and oil. Polish with a dry cloth. Greasy brass must first be scrubbed with soapsuds or sal soda solution before using special brass polish. The acid application is used to remove the tarnish. Rotten-stone takes up the superfluous acid and completes the polishing process. If this second process is not thorough the brass soon tarnishes again.

CARE OF GRANITE WARE

Granite ware utensils should be placed in a cold solution of soda in the proportion of one-half cup soda to one quart of water. They should be brought to a boil and boiled for an hour, or until the dirt rinses off readily, and then rinsed in the sink with clear water. If the stain is not removed scour utensils with bath-brick or sapolio. In emptying the strong soda water from the kettle in which utensils were boiled, be careful to pour through a funnel directly into the sink drain. Otherwise the soda will act on the metal of which the sink-plug is made.

CLEANING NICKEL WARE

Nickel can be kept bright by washing with hot soapsuds and wiping dry. If it needs polishing use a paste made by mixing whiting with ammonia. The paste should be about the consistency of milk, and should be applied with a flannel cloth and rubbed well into the crevices. Let it dry, then rub off the whiting and polish with a dry woolen cloth. There is an excellent prepared nickel polish on the market.

Badly stained nickel can be cleaned by boiling it in vinegar and alum mixture until stains begin to disappear, then polishing it again. The directions for making vinegar and alum mixture are as follows:

Vinegar and alum mixture:

2 oz. powdered alum.

1 qt. strong vinegar.

Boil the vinegar. Add the alum and stir until dissolved. Apply hot. If the nickel has become badly stained, it may be boiled in the mixture before it is polished. Boil until the stains begin to disappear. Mixture should be kept in a tightly corked bottle.

CLEANING SILVER

These directions apply only to the bright silver finish. Burnished silver should not be cleaned with any chemical. There are several methods.

1. Place the articles to be cleaned in a large aluminum kettle. Cover with boiling water in

which is dissolved one heaping tablespoonful of baking soda and one tablespoonful of salt to every quart of water. Let it come to a boil and boil five minutes. Rinse and wipe dry. Forty pieces of silver may be cleaned in this way in twenty minutes.

2. Use scrap zinc in an agate ware dish, the same solution and the same method.

3. In small families there need be no weekly cleaning of silver if a small bottle of whiting be kept on the sink shelf and each piece rubbed up as needed, in connection with the dish-washing process. The method of cleaning silver with whiting is to dampen a cloth and dip it in the whiting, rubbing the silver over with it. When the whiting has dried, rub it off with another soft cloth and polish with chamois skin. For ornamental work use an old tooth-brush. Egg-stained or badly tarnished silver should be rubbed over with salt before applying the whiting.

CLEANING ZINC

Rub with a flannel cloth moistened with a little kerosene or use scourine or Dutch Cleanser to take off the spots. Then polish with a mixture of vinegar and alum.

CLEANING STEEL KNIVES AND FORKS

Scour with powdered bath-brick, using a cork dipped in oil or water, and then into the powdered

Reprinted from "The Healthful Farmhouse," by Helen Dodd, through the courtesy of the publishers, Whitcomb & Barrows

Well planned farm kitchenette. Sink close to stove. Slide connecting with dining-room above drain board

bath-brick. Steel knives that are to be packed
away for some time ought to be very carefully
dried before putting away.

DAILY CARE OF THE KITCHEN STOVE

The gas stove should be brushed clean with a
small brush and wiped over with a cloth dipped in
linseed oil.   The oil should be used very sparingly.
Use a few drops only on a flannel cloth.   This small
amount will penetrate the cloth thoroughly if left
over night.   And a cloth so prepared remains in
good service for two weeks, at the end of which time
it should be washed out in strong suds, dried and
given a new application of oil.   Being inflammable
it should be kept in a tin box when not in use.   The
drip pan under the gas burners should be washed
when necessary.   With careful management this
need not be done more than once a week.

The coal range must not be cleaned while it is
hot.   Let it cool down while you are at breakfast
or dinner.   After the dishes are washed brush the
stove clean of crumbs, dust, ashes, etc.   Dampen
the stove-cloth slightly with kerosene and rub up
the top of the stove and all nickel parts with this.
Many of the best housekeepers never use blacking
on the top of the stove.   This prevents the staining
of flat-irons and utensils with stove-blacking.

DAILY CARE OF THE KITCHEN FLOOR

If the floor is covered with linoleum the daily
care in most cases is just brushing up with a long-

handled mop. Where there are creeping children who occasionally find their way into the kitchen it is better to mop up the linoleum daily, using a dampened floor-cloth only, just to remove the dust.

The cold closet and refrigerator ought to be gone over every day and all left-over food disposed of, either included in the menus of the next few days or thrown away. If care is taken in the marketing and adapting each day's recipes to the size of the family, there will be very little left-over food to trouble one.

It is a good rule to cook just enough to go round of certain things that are not good warmed over, to cook double quantities of foods that are just as good the second day, and always to have an abundant supply of the essentials, such as bread, milk, eggs and fruit. If a family is fond of cake and cookies, always keep plenty of these on hand. Where there is an abundance of the essentials it is not noticed if there is only one baked potato to go around, or one serving of any special delicacy.

The whole secret of wise kitchen management is to keep your kitchen and utensils so clean all the time that there will not need to be any grand "clarin' up spells"; to cook the more permanent supplies in quantity, and to carefully adjust the menus to the daily consumption, so as not to be bothered with "left-overs" in amounts that are only a nuisance.

The sanitary care of the kitchen includes special attention to the containers of food. They should be scalded out and sunned once a week in ordinary weather, and two or three times a week in hot weather. The refrigerator, cold closet, bread and cake boxes should all receive daily care. The sanitary care of garbage is discussed in Chapter XII.

XIV

THE LAUNDRY PROBLEM

THE consideration of the laundry problem does not properly belong to a study of the kitchen and its equipment. We strongly recommend taking all such work out of the kitchen and making provision for it in some other way. The kitchen is no place for laundry work. Had housekeepers realized this long ago, coöperative laundries would have flourished. Or at least we should have had wash-houses for neighborhood work, where each family might have, once a week, the use of a room and suitable laundry equipment.

In many homes where the stationary laundry tubs have been located in the kitchen, it is possible to have them taken out and placed in the basement or to have a small laundry built at the rear of the kitchen. This plan is recommended wherever it is possible to make the change. In every case where it has been done, the housekeeper is enthusiastic over the added convenience.

In building a new house it is desirable to make the kitchen small and to build the laundry next to it on the same floor. The room need not be large, but it ought to have good light and a place for stationary or portable tubs and for an ironing board that is always in position for work. (See Fig. 37.) A small closet to hold the laundry equipment is also a necessity. The chemicals for removing stains should be kept on the top shelf of this closet. Javelle water, borax, ammonia, oxalic acid and common table salt are the ones most frequently used. The wash-boiler may be heated on a small laundry stove which also heats the supply of hot water for the kitchen, or on a two-burner gas plate stove which can be located in the laundry. Such a room is valuable even if washing is never done at home, as it is a place where clothing may be brushed and cleaned and where clothes may be pressed whenever necessary. It is a great advantage to have a 6-inch shelf fastened to the wall, on which the tan and white shoes of the family may be left when drying, and where the blacking and shoe-cleaning materials may be kept.

When one lives in a rented house and cannot assume the expense of changing the location of the laundry tubs, it is the part of wisdom to reduce as much as possible the amount of washing to be done in the kitchen. This is done by sending to the laundry all the "flat work." Fine table linen and bed linen cannot safely be sent out, but the ordinary grades are done very satisfactorily and at moderate price. The gain in reducing the volume of washing is also felt on rainy days when it is a problem to dry the clothes.

The invention of the electric iron has made it

possible to have the ironing done outside the kitchen
even if the washing must still be carried on there.
Housekeepers who cannot change the tubs will
often be able to fit up a little upstairs room for the
ironing. In this room all the equipment for ironing should be kept, the ironing board, the sleeve
board, wax, iron, clothes-horse, cheese-cloth or
paper toweling for pressing, a heavy Turkish
towel for ironing embroidered pieces and a hamper
to hold the clean clothes before they are dampened
and folded for ironing. Such a room will have
many of the advantages of the specially built laundry.

Wise housekeepers are able greatly to reduce the
amount of ironing to be done by purchasing the
kind of underclothing and shirt-waists that do not
require ironing. There is abundant selection of
such things now to choose from, including knitted
underwear, crinkled seersucker garments and crepe
waists and dresses. Small Turkish towels may be
substituted for linen and huck towels, and paper toweling for kitchen and bathroom use reduces both the
amount of washing and ironing. The idea in this
case, as in so many others, is to study out the special
conditions that affect the washing and ironing problem differently in each individual family and make
such a solution of them that you will secure the best
results with the minimum of care and anxiety.
Buy the right kind of things and make arrangements
to have an abundance of clean clothing, even if it

is not ironed, and then have everything that needs careful ironing given the expert attention that it needs. To secure these results with peace of mind you will need the following outfit of labor-saving equipment.

LABOR-SAVING LAUNDRY EQUIPMENT

Of the three chief labor-savers for the laundry, the most important is the electric iron.

A good electric iron for family use weighs six pounds, and should be connected with undetachable cord at its base. It takes an electrician to determine whether an electric iron is well made. Therefore this implement should not be bought on the advice of some irresponsible agent, or because it looks all right. It should be of a reliable make. A poorly constructed iron that is always getting out of order may cost so much in repairs that it would pay to throw it away and buy a good one. Furthermore, it always gives out just when you need it most, and cannot be repaired except by sending for an electrician. For all these reasons it is important to have a serviceable implement or none at all. An electric iron of the best type costs $5.00.

The using of an electric iron has many advantages:

1. If used in the kitchen it does not interfere with the use of the cook-stove.

2. It saves the time and energy spent in walking to and from the stove to re-heat the ordinary iron.

3. It acts as a sort of pace-maker to maintain a rapid rate of work. As it is easier to keep up to the pace of the iron than to constantly turn the current on or off, the natural tendency is to accelerate one's rate of work.

4. It makes it possible to do the ironing whenever it is most convenient, instead of selecting the time when the fire in the range is at its best, or when the exigencies of cooking permit.

5. It enables the worker to choose a cool location for her work, since the electricity does not affect the temperature of the room.

6. Ironing may be done sitting down if a stool of the right height is kept on hand.

7. It is very convenient for pressing the garments of the family, especially summer dresses.

8. The cost is negligible, since an electric iron soon pays for itself in the time it saves.

THE VACUUM WASHER

While electric washing machines are a great comfort in any home where they can be afforded, and a necessity and economy in large families, they are, generally speaking, beyond the average means. No one, however, need be without some form of serviceable washing machine, since excellent small vacuum washers are now on the market, at prices ranging from $1.50 up to $6.00. The advantage of these small machines is that they can be used with any outfit. They are equally adaptable to set tubs or portable tubs. Most of them give best results when used in connection with a boiler placed on a laundry stove of the right height. The washer is used while the clothes are in the boiler on the stove, and the temperature is thus maintained at a higher degree than would be possible in the tubs. After the first boilerful of clothes is finished, the clothes are put through the rinse water, and the washer is used also in the rinsing. These washers are invaluable in emergencies and for washing blankets, which one dare not send out unless one knows of exceptional laundries or cleaning establishments.

In well-appointed laundries the ironing-board rests on an iron foot which supports it firmly, extending part way under the board so that it is kept firm and immovable. Such ironing-boards cost about $15.

The same result can be secured in the private home by an ingenious method of fastening the board at one end to the side wall of the room by hinges. When in use it is firmly supported. At other times it is_ folded back against the wall. Figure 37 shows how such an arrangement looks both in position for use and when folded back. If desirable it may be enclosed in a wall cupboard when not in use. With this and an electric iron it is possible to do the ironing in any room that may be conveniently used for this purpose, and the outfit is always ready for immediate use. It is made by fastening a strip of wood one inch thick and three inches wide to the

under side of the ironing board by means of a hinge.
A strap hinge fastens the ironing-board itself to a
brace on the wall. When in position the leg rests

Fig. 37.— Ironing board, which, when not
in use, can be folded back into a shallow cupboard built in for it.

against the wall. When folded up the board is
fastened to the side-wall by means of a hook and
eye.

A Clothes Boiler of copper, or at least with copper bottom and of the best grade of block tin, is
another desirable addition to the light laundry outfit. Used in connection with the vacuum washer,
or even where clothes are washed by the paraffine
method, it is indispensable. A very instructive
government bulletin gives directions for fitting a

bottom to this boiler, making it a valuable utensil for canning fruit and vegetables. While it cannot be considered a necessity for light laundry work, as can the three appliances already described, it is a most valuable and useful addition to the laundry equipment, and a necessity when clothes are washed by the ordinary method.

Three portable, galvanized iron tubs (where station-
 ary tubs are not installed) $3.75
Clothes stick (an old broom-stick with rounded ends)
Three dozen clothes-pins and clothes-pin bag or
 basket .... .75
Clothes line. The best kind is rope. Keep in a bag
 when not in use. Cost per 100 feet .... .65
Six-foot piece of rubber hose, ¾ inch size, fitted at
 one end with screw threads to attach to faucet.
 Saves all trouble in filling portable tubs .... .60
Enameled ware dish pan for washing out small
 pieces, or for use in starching, or carrying
 clothes back and forth from the boiler .... .75
Clothes horse 1.50
Clothes basket 1.25
                                                  ─────
                                                  $9.25

In addition to the above special laundry equipment, certain kitchen utensils are necessary, and may be borrowed from the regular kitchen outfit for occasional use. If washing is done regularly at home, it will be better to buy a separate set of the following articles:

Enameled saucepan, capacity 5 to 6 qts., for making
 starch ....$ .50
Tea-kettle, enamel ware .... .75
1 tablespoon (for measuring and stirring) .... .50
1 teaspoon (for measuring and stirring) .... .05
1 agate or tin measuring cup .... .05
1 quart measure .... .15
                                                  ─────
                                                  $2.00

With such an outfit it is possible to be quite independent of the laundry question. One can send
the entire washing out, or part of it out, or have it
all done at home.   It is perfectly possible to do one
thing one week and try another the next without
serious adjustment.   The expense of the outfit is
not large, and in these transition days, when the old
resources are failing and the new ones have not
become fully established, it is the part of wisdom to
be fully prepared for any emergency.

XV

The Business Side of the Kitchen

EVEN more important than the work of the kitchen is the business side of the kitchen. This involves such an orderly record of costs, of work done and experience gained, as will serve as a guide in administering the family budget, and finally in achieving the results which are the object and goal of all effort toward real home-making.

The business management of the kitchen falls logically into three main divisions: The keeping of accounts; the purchasing and care of supplies; and the keeping of kitchen records. The last includes favorite recipes and useful memoranda, more especially the sort of information that cannot be found in books or libraries. Of such are data relating to new and untried equipment; addresses and exact names of reliable tradesmen, valuable equipment or desirable brands of supplies; memoranda of the particular needs in your special circumstances, which perhaps, as they may not apply to any other conditions, will never find their way into print.

Account-keeping for the home is made exceedingly simple nowadays because the whole business world is organized on one of two systems, either that of cash payments or monthly settlements. Accounts cannot be allowed to run on and on indefinitely as they did a few years ago. Frequent settlements at regular intervals make it easy for the housekeeper to form the habit of paying bills at a certain time each month, and making out a monthly statement of the various ways in which the money has been spent.

In learning to live wisely on a given income, the first step is to make in advance a theoretical budget apportioning one's income as seems best to the various departments of living expense. Then keep track of the actual expenses, and compare the amounts spent with the theoretical budget decided upon. It often happens that what seems best in theory does not work out well in practice. After a few months' experience it is possible to make a division that is much better suited to the individual need.

For instance, economists have worked out an apportionment of income which is a safe guide for most housekeepers as a starting-point: So much for rent; so much for operating expense; so much for food, for clothing, for the "higher life," etc. But when one attempts to actually make this apportionment, it is often found to be impossible to maintain the standard of living and keep within the prescribed limits. Original thinking is therefore necessary in applying these standard percentages to individual and special conditions. In working out a wise apportionment of income, no one thing is so valuable as a careful record of what the daily living *actually costs.* Therefore a simple system of monthly account-keeping must be adopted by every family. The system should not require too much work. But, to be effective it should keep track of every important detail.

The best and simplest system that we know has been used at the Housekeeping Experiment Station for nine years. It never takes more than ten minutes to jot down in a small cash-book the daily cash expenses; or more than two hours a month to check up the totals of the monthly statements of the tradesmen with the order slips, make out the checks and balance the check-book. Although in several instances bills have been presented that have already been paid, it has always been possible to locate without delay the necessary receipt. In one case it was necessary to find a receipt for china purchased three years before the duplicate bill came in. The labor of hunting up the envelope containing the record of this purchase required exactly ten minutes.

The system has one inflexible requirement which, like the laws of the Medes and Persians, "changeth not." That is to deposit in the bank *all the money that comes into the family till,* whether it is salary or dividends, an unlooked-for windfall or merely a birthday present. The amount of the deposit is entered in the left-hand column of the ruled page of the check book opposite the checks. Together with the entry a memorandum is also made stating the source, or any necessary information relating to the deposit. Each deposit, added to the amount of money already in the bank, shows the total amount that has been deposited. The right-hand column of this blank page in the check-book shows a corresponding record of all money paid out. Each check stub should give the name of the person or firm to whom the check is made payable, and a memorandum of what it is for, as clothing, coal, etc. At the foot of the page a total is taken of the income column and the expense column. The difference between the two represents the amount of cash actually on hand. This balance is carried forward to the top of the income column of the next page.

We keep our record with the bank just as carefully as if it depended upon us alone to know whether or not the balance is correct, and we check up our balance with the bank every month or two. Usually the bank balance is larger than ours, because several checks which we have drawn have not yet been presented for payment. To make a list of the checks which have not been returned we place a blue pencil check mark opposite each check stub that has come back. Then we take the number and amount of the stubs which have no mark after them and deduct the total of these from the balance shown by the bank book.   This gives us the " true balance " and should be exactly the same amount as our check book balance shows at that date.

It is exceedingly easy, however, to make a mistake in addition, to forget to put down a deposit, or even to make out a check and forget to fill in the stub.   So it sometimes happens that we have to go over our entries very carefully and check up each with the bank record, and then go over the totals to see whether we have made an error in addition or subtraction.   It usually happens that the mistake has been made by the housekeeper and not by the bank.   The bank *must* be accurate and balance up its cash to a cent each day in order to transact its business.   If the bank makes mistakes, it is a pretty reliable sign that its business is not being well done, and that it is not a safe institution to have dealings with.   Reasoning of this kind once caused us to withdraw our account from a bank which had a high reputation for stability, but which had made a mistake of several dollars in its balance.   The bank failed a few months later.   It was discovered that its funds had been used for speculation for several years and its methods had become lax.   One cannot be too careful nowadays in the matter of accurately keeping accounts.

In addition to the check-book, which is our complete record of all family expenses, we have only to keep a small cash-book for certain items that are too small to pay by check. The cash account is made part of the check-book system by simply drawing a weekly cash check to cover the amount we think we shall need. The total of this check is entered on the left hand side of the cash-book. Every item of expense paid out is entered on the right. We try to group the expenses as we go along because the record is of value to us just in proportion to the training it gives us. For instance, suppose we spend $5 on a trip to the city. Our entries may read like this as we jot them down at the end of the day:

```
June 15. Carfare ........................$ .05
         Ticket  .........................  .60
         Lunch  ..........................  .40
         Telephone  ......................  .10
         Ribbons  ........................ 1.25
         Hat  ............................ 2.00
         Ticket  .........................  .60
                                          _____
                                          $5.00
```

Or it may read:

```
June 15. Trip to the city ................$1.75
         Clothing  ....................... 3.25
                                          _____
              Total  ............$5.00
```

In the former case we have not taken pains to separate the expense of the trip itself, which would always be practically the same, from the amount spent for clothing. The record is over-loaded with detail and gives no information of value. In the latter, we have analyzed the account. This analyzing of items soon becomes a habit; and it is the most helpful habit that we can cultivate now-a-days when conserving the income is only possible through an exact knowledge of values. The old idea of *economy in everything* is being replaced by definite knowledge of *what not to do*. Certain expenses inevitably follow certain decisions and cannot be controlled. Therefore our account-keeping rescues us from many difficult positions, and enables us to know with certainty what we can do and what we ought to avoid.

The cash account, then, is kept exactly as is the check account. At the bottom of each page a total is taken of the amount of cash drawn out; and of the expenses on the opposite page. The difference between the two represents the cash on hand and is brought forward to the next page. At the end of the month the expenses are grouped under the proper heads, such as clothing, wages, food, etc., and added to the amount spent for these items through checks. This gives us a complete record of the various ways in which money has been spent, and is one of the chief objects for which accounts have been kept. .The totals are filed on a card and can be compared at any time with the expenses of a previous month. In this way we learn to spend our income to the best advantage, to protect ourselves from other people's carelessness, and always to discriminate intelligently between what

" it were good to do " and what we are financially able to do.

PURCHASING SUPPLIES

Each department of household expense has its own problems and must be dealt with, in the light of experience, in such a manner as to get the best results. In this book we shall consider one department only, that relating to the needs and requirements of the kitchen.

In order to get the best value for the money expended for food supplies, the housekeeper may pursue one of two general policies, either of which, intelligently followed up, gives good results.

The French system consists of buying in very small quantities as food is needed. By this plan we pay a slightly higher price, but avoid the care of storage, the risk of deterioration and all temptation to careless or wasteful use that comes with having abundant reserve supplies on hand. Very many housekeepers have no choice in the matter, since those who must move often or live in apartments cannot store anything not absolutely necessary to be kept on hand. For this very large class of home-makers we recommend our Standard List, which is given on pages 209 and 210, and which amply provides for both the daily needs and for emergencies.

The other plan is to buy in quantity and thus obtain a substantial reduction in price. For housekeepers who live in the country and can have a good cold storage cellar, it will pay to make a practice of buying not only groceries and canned foods in quantity, but the winter supply of vegetables, apples, oranges and grape-fruit. It may even be an advantage to put down eggs in water glass if one lives in a community where eggs ever get as low as 20 to 25 cents a dozen.

It is important, however, to know both how to select and how to care for food in storage. The cold cellar must be properly ventilated, and also protected from excessive cold. One must know how to choose a satisfactory grade of supplies that will keep. Fruit and vegetables must be frequently gone over and all decayed articles removed. At least an hour a week should be given to this work by the householder in person, since one cannot entrust it to an ordinary maid or leave reserve supplies open to careless use.

If this plan is carried out in connection with a home garden it will prove a great economy. With good management a moderate-sized garden plot will yield a great part of all the vegetables a family needs for winter use, and many of the fruits and vegetables for canning. The labor of caring for such a garden is not great, and is better worth while than any other department of home work that we have, since it keeps the whole family out of doors and happily occupied.

KEEPING TRACK OF SUPPLIES

Whatever purchasing system may be adopted,

whether supplies are bought in quantity or in small amounts as needed, it is important that the renewing be done in a methodical way. In the entire realm of home economics there is no more prolific source of wasted time and energy than that caused by a hand-to-mouth habit of buying.

Let us suppose that the cook or housekeeper is all ready to make a batch of apple pies. At the last moment she discovers that there is no lard in the house or no nutmeg. Then ensues a hurried trip to the corner grocery. Or perhaps a telephone order must be sent and the cooking delayed until the goods arrive. Probably it is a late hour of the morning when everybody is telephoning, and the line is busy. As a result of this lack of foresight twice as much time is consumed as the actual cooking operation requires. The work is done in an atmosphere of worry and confusion and the whole morning's schedule is thrown out of focus.

At the Housekeeping Experiment Station we avoid all this by merely keeping a pad and pencil hung up in the kitchen on which orders are made out in advance. We plan to keep a certain amount of supplies on hand to cover daily needs and emergency needs. Whenever a can is used a memo at once goes on the pad to replace it. When the tea canister or coffee canister gets down to two-thirds a new supply is purchased. We never wait for anything to be actually gone before replacing it. We telephone orders once, twice or three times a week as the need requires, trying to consider the convenience of the grocer as well as our own and not to ask unnecessary deliveries.

No great amount of storage space is needed for a supply such as we recommend. At the Experiment Station the supply is kept in the kitchenette itself, a room 6 ft. 6 by 11. There is no regular storage pantry, but the east wall of the kitchenette is fitted up with open shelves above the work table on which we keep all articles needed for daily use and emergencies. The amount of money needed to purchase the given list is also small; and the added efficiency through time saved in the planning and preparation of meals is very great. This, therefore, is one of the wise investments for housekeepers of small means as well as those of abundant income.

STANDARD LIST OF KITCHEN SUPPLIES

Granulated sugar ..	5 lbs.	Molasses	1 qt.
Lump sugar	1 "	Flour:	
Powdered sugar ...	1 "	Bread ....25 lbs.	
Brown sugar	1 "	Pastry ....10 "	
Coffee	1 "	Graham .... 5 "	
Tea	1 "	Rye .... 1 "	
Baking powder	1 "	Cereals:	
Corn starch	1 pkg.	Oatmeal .... 3 "	
Cream tartar ......¼ lb.		Hominy .... 1 "	
Baking soda	1 lb.	Unpolished rice .. 3 "	
Tapioca	1 pkg.	Yellow corn meal 1 "	
Eggs	1 doz.	2 kinds of un-	
Butter	2 lbs.	cooked cereals.	
Lard	3 "	Macaroni .... 1 pkg.	
Lemons .... 3 to 6			

Canned Goods:

Corn .... 2 cans
Peas .... 2 "
Shrimp .... 2 "
Tomatoes ...... 2 "
Salmon .... 2 "
Peaches .... 2 "
Cherries .... 2 "
Plum pudding ... 2 "
Chicken .... 2 "
Shredded codfish 1 lb.
Dried beef..2 glass jars

Bacon ....3 lb. strip
6 Beef tablets.
Currants .... 1 pkg.
Small can pimentoes.
Evaporated cream 2 cans
Sardines .... 2 "
Stuffed olives....2 bottles
Seeded raisins .. 1 pkg.
Grated pineapple. 1 can
Hawaiian pineapple.

Soup Flavorings:

Salt.
White pepper .... 1 can
Pepper corns..5c. worth
Bay leaves .... " "
Clove .... " "
Thyme .... " "

Marjoram ....5c. worth
Celery .... " "
Onion extract.
Evaporated carrots.1 lb.
Celery salt.
Evaporated turnips.1 lb.

Condiments and Seasonings:

Extract of Vanilla.
"   " Lemon.
"   " Almond.
Salad materials:
Paprika ....1 can
Garlic cloves...5c. worth

Tarragon vinegar...
...............1 bottle
Olive oil ....1 gal.
Cider vinegar ......1 qt.
Mustard ....1 can

Spices:

Cinnamon.
Ginger.
Mace.

All-spice.
Nut-meg.
Red pepper.

Miscellaneous:

Poultry seasoning.
Imitation maple syrup
   extract.
Currie powder.
Gelatin ....2 pkgs.
Refined cotton seed oil.

Dried apricots.......1 lb.
" prunes ......" "
" mushrooms .." "
3 lbs. Milk crackers.
1 lb. Saltines.

The housekeeper who arranges to keep on hand a Standard List like the foregoing can avoid the most prolific sources of worry, delay and wasted energy. An orderly method of keeping track of supplies soon becomes a habit. Mechanically, almost without thought, needs are jotted down in advance. The day's orders are telephoned at a convenient hour before the line gets busy. Best of all her day can be planned to the best advantage, and she is never at the mercy of fate when emergencies arise.

ORDERING SUPPLIES

A strong prejudice against ordering by telephone has developed in the past few years, some authorities even going so far as to charge up against the telephone the entire responsibility for the high cost of living!

It is true that serious abuses are possible in homes where supplies are carelessly telephoned for by anybody and everybody, without any subsequent checking up. Nevertheless, in spite of sensational warnings against the practice, there is much to be said in its favor. The evils of the system have crept in through ignorance or lack of training on the part of the housekeeper and dishonesty on the part of the merchant. As neither the one nor the other defect is inevitable, there is no reason why either should be permitted to discredit a convenience that, properly used, may be quite as valuable to the housekeeper as to the business man.

Housekeepers are realizing that they must learn how to purchase wisely, and that a knowledge of the reliable brands of food is part of the education necessary to successful home-making. Everywhere courses in marketing and food values are being given to women's clubs. Merchants are being called to account for dishonest dealing and are suffering loss of trade if they persist in taking advantage of ignorance. On the other hand those who can be trusted to properly fill orders are meeting deserved success. Where the housekeeper knows her end of the business and the merchant can be relied on, the use of the telephone means a great saving of time and energy at both ends of the wire. Competent market men, for example, know more about meats than the average housekeeper can learn in a lifetime. If this knowledge can be enlisted in the interest of the home, and if the housekeeper is willing to pay the slightly higher price such honest and intelligent service is worth, the use of the telephone will be the greatest possible benefit.

When all is said and done, it is simply a problem in mathematics. Conditions vary in different communities, and the only way to test them is by experiment. Let the housekeeper first try going to market for a month, keeping a careful record of the time and car fare consumed by this method. Then, when she knows the market conditions, and the best places to purchase to advantage, let her select a reliable butcher and grocer and a good place to buy fruit and vegetables. Let her give her orders by telephone at a certain regular time each day, and carry out this plan also for a month, carefully comparing the results of the two systems one with the other. She can then readily judge which is the better plan in her particular case. She may find that marketing once a week and paying cash prices, combined with the telephone system for other days, will be more effective than either plan for her needs. If the family is large and the children grown up, the money saved by cash marketing may far out-weigh every other consideration. The question may be decided by each individual on its merits, since able housekeepers have proved it is possible to get the right kind of supplies by either method.

CHECKING UP SUPPLIES

In Chapter IV on *Built-in Conveniences* we have spoken of the importance of having a shelf or closet at the back entrance to receive daily supplies as they are left by the tradesmen. Near this closet should be hung a bill clip, so that the slips accompanying each order may be checked up before the goods are put away, and the slips placed in the clip until the end of the month. The total amount on the slips should then be checked up with the total of the monthly statement. If any mistake has been made in the order, any wrong charge or any shortage of goods, or if the goods themselves were unsatisfactory, the dealer has been called up at the time of delivery, and the matter corrected. A note of the correction has been made on the slip. Credit slips are kept with the charge slips, so that everything can be quickly checked and verified before making out the check.

Tradesmen who do not have telephones are given instructions to leave a certain order of bread, eggs, or what not, daily or weekly. If any change is made, a note is left near where the goods are delivered, giving the necessary instructions to increase or reduce the order. If slips are not left with the orders, a card is nailed up against the wall, on which each delivery is marked. At the end of the week or the end of the month the amounts are totaled up and paid. We have a general understanding with all dealers that as long as they leave us first-class goods we make no change in the order, but that any inferior or imperfect goods will be returned. We pay promptly and make a point of giving a certain definite amount of trade that can be counted on. In this way we get the best service with the least expenditure of our own time and effort.

THE KITCHEN RECORDS

In order that the best methods may be carried out in the kitchen, and that the one who does the work may have in available form the recipes, menus and directions relating to the various details of her business, it is necessary to have some place in the

Home-made kitchen cabinet. Making the most of limited
wall space. Pastry board pulls out beneath
one of the shelves

kitchen in which may be kept a complete set of reference cards for kitchen records.

Very few home-makers realize how much time is lost through failure to keep accurate, tested recipes adapted to the size of the family, in a convenient place and ready for constant reference. Somewhere in most houses this information is stored, but it is not available when needed. Very much of the cooking, for example, is done by guess-work. More food is prepared than is needed, and is then either wasted or requires special thought and care to warm over.

There is a very simple way of controlling the situation. Make out for kitchen use a set of card recipes of all foods used contantly, even including cereals. Adapt these rules to the number of persons in the family. Keep the cards alphabetically indexed in a small oak box which sells for 75 cents. Such a box is technically known as a " jogger." A 4 by 6 card is the best size for the purpose, and it should be of a good grade of card-board. Each recipe card ought to contain the following information:

1. List of necessary ingredients.
2. Directions for mixing.
3. Directions for baking, with exact baking temperatures and exact time required for baking.
4. Number of persons rule will serve.
5. Exact time required for mixing.
6. Cost of materials.

The following shows a tested recipe card with full directions:

RYE MUFFINS

1 cup rye flour;	1 cup milk;
1 cup white flour;	1 egg;
¼ cup sugar;	1 tablespoon melted butter;
1 teaspoonful salt;	4 teaspoons baking powder.

1. Mix and sift dry ingredients. Add gradually the milk, egg well beaten and melted butter.

2. Heat oven to a temperature of 420 degrees F.* by turning on both burners for about seven minutes, using thermometer to test. Turn both burners as low as possible to maintain this temperature. Place muffins on lower shelf and bake for 20 minutes. They should be well raised by this time and commence to brown. Turn on heat full for 5 to 7 minutes, when muffins will be well browned and ready to take out.

3. Rule makes 12 muffins.

4. 6 minutes are required for mixing.

5. Material costs 10 cents.

Such a record is valuable for the following reasons:

1. It enables one to perform the work in the shortest possible time.

2. It is possible to see at a glance the special conditions governing each single operation, so that a person of intelligence may be able to group to best advantage a number of tasks that may need to be watched up at the same time.

3. It prevents wasting time in looking up details that cannot safely be trusted to the memory.

4. It assures perfectly cooked food and therefore prevents waste of valuable materials.

* Where thermometers are not used directions for paper tests may be substituted.

5. The baking temperatures worked out for one kind of food as a rule apply to all recipes of the same class. Thus the directions for rye muffins apply to all other kinds of muffins, and need not be repeated.

6. It prevents small amounts of different kinds of food being left over, to either be wasted or take time and thought to serve again in some palatable form.

7. It is a valuable record that can be used by any one as a guide for the same kind of work. Details slip from the memory, and a careful habit of making and preserving records is the greatest asset that any home-maker can have.

Another serious loss of time, resulting also in much damage to valuable property, is caused by failure to keep careful directions for the care of equipment. The cleaning of metals, care of hardwood, etc., are important tasks. Yet either no directions at all are given for their performance, or it must be given verbally to each new maid or outside houseworker who comes in. Such directions should be recorded on cards and kept in a convenient place in the kitchen for constant reference. Any housekeeper can make a set of these cards for herself by purchasing strong bond letter paper 7 by 11. Or the directions may be written on heavy cards 5 by 8 in size.

The Housekeeping Experiment Station has in

preparation a complete set of Kitchen Record Cards which will be issued in a short time for the use of home-makers. These cards will have the directions printed in clear type, and each card will have a hole by which it may be suspended from a hook where it can be easily seen by the person performing the work.

XVI

The Home-maker's Quiet Corner

THIS little book has been written in vain if it has not been made abundantly clear that the business of real home-making is a problem for heart and brain rather than one demanding mere physical toil for its solution.

However necessary it may be for the mother of a family to master the practical details of her business, it is, in the final analysis, an administrative problem. Therefore the Efficient Kitchen will fall far short of its purpose unless the home-maker can have somewhere in the house a quiet corner where she can be free to do the thinking and planning necessary to coördinate the household machinery and make it run effectively.

The Quiet Corner corresponds to the business man's office. It should if possible be a separate little room away from noise and interruptions, and should be conveniently fitted up with writing table, book-shelves and files. Here the day's work is planned, accounts are kept and the indispensable housekeeping records are made and filed away in convenient form for handy reference.

The cost of fitting up such an adjunct to the

Efficient Kitchen may be anywhere from about $10 to $150. But whether the expense be much or little, the equipment should be *of the right kind.* The " jigglely " little " ladies' desks " that look so ornamental are the wrong kind. Much to be preferred is a plain kitchen table with two drawers, which may be purchased unstained for $2.50. Ten dollars will buy a very complete outfit including a

Fig. 38.— Least expensive equipment for the Homemaker's Quiet Corner.

kitchen table and chair to match, a scrap basket, scissors, two letter files and a good supply of paper, pencils, memorandum pads, etc. (See Fig. 38.) The table and chair may be stained oak, green or cherry to match their surroundings.

We have already spoken of the advantage of a card system for the kitchen records in constant use. These kitchen records will be merely part of a general card and filing system covering all departments of the household needs, to be made out, consulted and filed in the Home-maker's Quiet Corner. The family account-keeping, for example, is very simple and consists of comparatively few items. Nevertheless it covers an immense amount of detail. To tax the memory with a multitude of facts that, in themselves are unimportant, is a great mistake and has been a main cause of the terrible waste of energy seen in many homes. "Mother" is expected to be constantly at everybody's beck and call, and to be an encyclopedia of useful information for the entire family. She must not only remember the details that properly fall to her own work, but she must make good the shortcomings caused by carelessness of other members of the family. If she does not in self-defense adopt a simple and accurate system of keeping track of things she becomes a hopeless burden bearer.

We all know homes where the mother is constantly interrupting important work to hunt up some missing article for one member or another of the family; where hours are lost hunting for things that are needed but have been tucked away somewhere. No one can find them but "Mother" if she has put them away, and if she trusts to an over-burdened memory which fails her at the most critical times. If she has a system, however, she can say: "Your winter flannels are in the cedar chest in a package labeled 'T's Winter Flannels,'" or "The gloves are in the right-hand upper corner of my bureau drawer." Many women are naturally systematic and have worked out for themselves simple and effective ways of conserving their time. Many others have good memories and can always remember. These two classes of women need very little help; but there is a still larger class who are neither systematic nor gifted with good memories, but who would become the best kind of home-makers if they would carry out a systematic plan of keeping records of all information by means of a card system.

We have spoken of the need of having accurate recipes and direction cards in the kitchen. This is the first step toward starting a valuable system which may be applied to other departments of the house-work. The next step is to get the " card habit " and free one's thought from all unnecessary detail. The two sizes of cards best adapted to the use of the home are 3 by 5 and 4 by 6. Card index trays, such as librarians use, come to fit in ordinary drawers. These index trays are about fifteen inches long. You start the system by writing out on an index card the subject you want to keep track of. These subjects may be: Household Accounts; Addresses, Personal and Business; Linen Supply; Miscellaneous Information. Then every fact that needs to be remembered may be written down on a card under its proper grouping. In a short time it becomes a habit to jot things down, and finally it becomes almost mechanical to keep track of every-thing by means of the cards.

When one or another needs to know where things are, or what kind and size of stockings to buy for John, or where you can get the best grade and size of bedding, you simply consult your card record, and save the time of looking up all these details. Until you begin to think about it you will not realize how much time you formerly wasted just because you failed to make unimportant matters automatic.

Duplicates of all recipe cards should be kept in the Quiet Corner; for it is here that you plan your meals, and here that it will be of most service to have recipes grouped in a suggestive way. For instance: you have under one grouping *Supper Dishes,* giving a list of the supper dishes that have been found best adapted to the tastes and need of the family. Another grouping is devoted to *Quickly Prepared Meals.* Another to *Emergency Dinners,* etc. These groupings come to you in the form of suggestions from friends or magazine articles. You jot them down, try them out, and add them, if found worthy, to your "tried and true" card recipe index. Often they cannot be duplicated because they have never been written down by any one before. For that reason one ought not to keep the original card in the kitchen, but should have a set of duplicates for kitchen use. It is also not necessary to have on the kitchen card all the detail that may be desirable for the permanent file. The cost of food and the time required to prepare it are needed when one *plans* the day's work. In the actual doing of it one has more need of baking directions, exact amounts of ingredients, etc.

The most important feature of the card system is to have a small oak " jogger " to be kept on one's desk to hold memoranda that will serve as a guide to the immediate day's work. Any special work for a certain day is written, say, on a card marked *Tuesday.* Perhaps Tuesday is the regular wash day; but bread must be set at night and peas soaked for Wednesday's pea soup. A glance at the card will serve as a reminder to maid or housekeeper. There are duties that change every day even though certain days are set apart for special tasks. These directions are written out as they are thought of, and each morning a card of special directions is given to the maid, together with the menus for the day. Perhaps the laundress comes once a week and you must remember to tell her. to take special pains ironing the fine white dress, to set the color in E's new gingham dresses, not to starch the curtains too much. So as these ideas occur to you they are written down on the Laundress' card. Another card is kept for the man who comes once a week to mow the lawn and do odd jobs about the house. You jot down on Brown's card:

Fix screens to cellar window.
Loosen library windows that stick.
Mow lawn.
Transplant iris.
New pane of glass in vestibule.

Suppose you happen to be out when Brown comes, or an unexpected caller arrives. It is not necessary to see him, or to tax your mind with the list of little things that will help in making the next week go smoothly. All you have to do about Brown is to leave the card for him.

In the same way a card keeps track of the errands that must be done next time we go to the city to shop. On it sizes, addresses, etc., are written down, so that these do not have to be specially remembered. All these cards are filed alphabetically so we can take them out of the " jogger " when we need them. As soon as a list is done with it is destroyed, and a new card started. If one or two items still remain to be attended to they are transferred to the new card.

The cost of card trays and joggers for both kitchen and Quiet Corner will be about $3.00. There will be two joggers, one holding 4 by 6 cards, and a smaller one for the desk holding 3 by 5 cards. There will be two card trays or oak drawers filled with index cards, one 4 by 6, for the original recipes kept in the office, and one tray fitted out with 3 by 5 cards for miscellaneous information.

The following memorandum shows the complete cost of fitting up the Quiet Corner (or Office as it is more prosaically called in many households) with the necessary furniture, filing arrangements, etc., required for making and keeping such household records as we recommend:

1. Least expensive outfit for the Quiet Corner:

Kitchen table, stained oak, cherry or green	$2.75
Scrap basket	.75
Ordinary chair to match table	1.00
Scissors	.25
Two letter files	.70
Pencils, paper, pads, etc.	1.50
Joggers and card trays as itemized above	3.00
Total	**$9.95**

Instead of the inexpensive letter files in the above list one may purchase two inexpensive vertical files resting on a base. It consists of two sections and the base, and sells for about $6.00. It is similar to the one illustrated on page 227. It is a great convenience in any home, as it keeps important papers and letters in the most compact and convenient shape.

At the Housekeeping Experiment Station we have a more elaborate equipment because our needs are both private and professional. The outfit is wonderfully complete and satisfactory, and is especially adapted to the needs of professional women, club women and teachers doing research work. It is illustrated on page 227. (See Fig. 39.) The filing cabinet contains hundreds of topics bearing on kitchen equipment, schools and their relation to the home, municipal problems, etc., etc. All this information has been gathered through personal experience and observation, or from newspapers and periodicals, and therefore cannot be found in any library. It is carefully indexed by means of the card system, and can be referred to at a moment's notice.

Our equipment, including a type-writer and type-writer desk, a revolving desk chair and the files,

FIG. 39.— A more elaborate "office" for the homemaker, thoroughly practical and desirable.

costs about $150. This will be found to be an investment that well pays for busy people.

We have spoken of the importance of having a separate room for the Home-maker's Quiet Corner. This may seem an impossible luxury to the unselfish housemother, who is apt to allow all needs to take precedence of her own. Yet peace and quiet at times are all-essential to the success of her work, and must by some means be secured.

We knew of one harassed mother of nine who now and again achieved a quiet hour in the midst of most wearisome toil, by donning a certain well-known sun-bonnet as a signal to the members of her household that she wished to be let alone!

Absurd and pathetic as this incident is, it nevertheless suggests a solution of the difficulty that is within the reach of all.

For the Home-maker's Quiet Corner, like much else that the new housekeeping stands for, is in reality a way of looking at things — an attitude of mind. If it is once clearly recognized that thinking and planning is the main business of home-making, and if all the household is taught to recognize this fact, it will not be difficult for the mother, whether or not she has a separate " office," to be as free from interruptions in her special corner of a bed-room or living-room, as if barricaded behind locked doors. The main thing is to make definite provision for the mental aspect and mental requirements of her work. Only through a right attitude, through recognizing the high importance of thought and intelligence in working out the household problems, is it possible to win through " villain kitchen vassalage " to glory.

GLOSSARY

The vocabulary of the new housekeeping is often a source of confusion to housekeepers. Unfamiliar words are used, or perfectly familiar words are used in a new sense. Certain technical or trade words are also necessary in describing processes or giving directions for construction.

Built-in-Conveniences.— As used in the Efficient Kitchen refers to shelf room, closets built into the wall, etc, and such other home-made contrivances as a carpenter can instal.

Cleat.— " A strip nailed or otherwise secured across a board, post, etc., for any purpose, as for supporting the end of a shelf " (Century Dictionary). In this book cleat means a narrow strip of wood nailed to the wall, from which brooms, mops, etc., may be suspended.

Fixed-Equipment.— Refers to the kind of equipment that must be permanently located, such as sink stove, etc.

Grill.— A flat perforated metal shelf to fit over the top of a steam or hot water radiator in kitchen or dining-room. Used for drying kitchen ware and keeping dishes warm in kitchen where there is no kitchen range.

Insulation.—" That state in which the communication of heat to other bodies is prevented by the interposition of a non-conductor: also the material or substance which insulates."

Pantry.— Technically "an apartment or closet in which provisions are kept or where plates and knives are cleaned." In this book the term refers to the small intervening room between kitchen and dining-room, often called "Butler's Pantry."

Radiator.— Defined in the Century Dictionary as "Anything which radiates: anything from which rays of heat emanate or radiate. Also a part of a heating apparatus designed to communicate heat to a room chiefly by convection but partly in some cases by radiation."

The term is used in The Efficient Kitchen to apply to the soap stone or iron discs which are used as the heating agents in fireless cook stoves. Also used to designate the steam or hot water coils used to heat a room.

Stove.— Defined in the Century Dictionary as "A closed or partly closed vessel or receiver in which fuel is burned, the radiated heat being used to warm a room or for cooking." In common usage the word "stove" and "range" are used interchangeably, but manufacturers of coal stoves and ranges make a technical distinction. A "stove" has the collar for the smoke-pipe in the top at the end opposite the firebox and has two oven doors on opposite sides. A "range" has the collar for the smoke-pipe at right angles to the firebox, in the middle of the top at the back, and has but one oven door.

Thermos Bottle.— A bottle having a double wall so insulated as to retain the heat or cold in the liquid placed in it.

Vent Valve.— A safety or poppet valve placed in the cover of a fireless cook stove to allow steam to escape when the pressure inside is sufficient to lift the valve. The valve makes roasting and baking possible, without the necessity of opening the cooker to release the surplus steam.

INDEX

235

CPSIA information can be obtained
at www.ICGtesting.com
Printed in the USA
BVHW040850180820
586419BV00013B/255